Voices and Poetry of Ireland

FOREWORD BY BRENDAN KENNELLY

HarperCollins*Publishers*

Voices and Poetry of Ireland

A collection of Ireland's best-loved poetry with recordings by Ireland's best-loved figures

HarperCollinsPublishers
77–85 Fulham Palace Road,
Hammersmith, London w6 8jb

www.harpercollins.co.uk

Published by HarperCollinsPublishers 2003
9 8 7 6 5 4 3 2 1

A catalogue record for this book
is available from the British Library

ISBN 0 00 717407 1

Designed by Geoff Green
Set in Monotype Baskerville

Printed and bound in Great Britain by
Butler & Tanner Ltd, Frome and London

Executive Producer: Brian Molloy
Producer/Co-Ordinator: Judy Cardiff
Assistant Co-Ordinator: Graham Molloy
Production & Recording engineer: Greg French
Mastering Engineer: Greg French

Contents

Foreword

Brian Molloy's inspired and inspiring idea of having a hundred well known Irish voices read a hundred poems by Irish poets has led to a unique three CD and book anthology which will reach readers and listeners throughout the world. This unique work, managed by Lunar Records and fully supported by Poetry Ireland, has the aim of raising badly needed funds for Focus Ireland, which works to alleviate and eliminate homelessness in this country. Focus Ireland was founded by Sister Stanislaus Kennedy in 1985. It is one of the largest voluntary agencies in the land, solely dedicated to combating homelessness. Every year, more than four thousand people are helped through the provisions of youth and outreach services, drop-in centres and hostels, and transitional and long-term housing facilities throughout Ireland. This marvellous anthology will enable the dedicated staff of Focus Ireland to do even greater work, and bring them closer to achieving their vision of an Ireland where everyone has a right to a place they can call home.

I call this anthology 'marvellous' and I mean exactly that. Here are some of the most moving, resonant, subtle and memorable voices ever to have come out of Ireland; and their voices are reading poems they love. When a voice reads a poem it loves, something unique happens. The voice brings the heart and mind, indeed the very soul of the listener into the complete act and art of listening, and a certain illuminating intensity electrifies the words in such a way that the poem's rhythm and music, meaning and movement, come together in a passionate oneness that is truly mesmeric and memorable. The human voice is an interpreter of meaning, but it is also a gentle, intense power that persuades the poem's inner music to flow confidently into the light and dark of the listener's being, linger there, plant the seeds of new insights, fresh ideas, and introduce the vibrant possibilities of a re-animated emotional life, a promise of genuine spiritual renewal. Some of the voices here are famous throughout the world, others are not so renowned, but all have something thrilling, thought-provoking and blood-stirring to offer. Each voice has its own special appeal. This book is a beautiful creation. Get it. And help Focus Ireland to fight the homelessness that poetry itself, in its own way, fights. These voices with their keen, loving sensitivity, these poems with their deep, unique music, unite to declare war on degrading poverty and to help deprived, lonely people find a home.

BRENDAN KENNELLY

Preface

Voices and Poetry of Ireland – matching them seems such a simple idea. It certainly was when I first got the notion over three years ago (January 1st 2000 to be precise). Voices have always been intriguing to me. I was drawn from my early boyhood, possibly because I was an only boy, to the enchantment of radio and the magical ability of voices to convey the wonders and excitement of life's broad tapestry. JFK, Mohammed Ali and our own Eamonn Andrews on *Sport Report*, Richard Burton, MacLiammoir – these and so many other voices had the power to add wings to flights of fancy not only for me but for so many others.

Little did I know when we, the wonderful Judy Cardiff and I, set off for the Taoiseach's office to make the first recording with Bertie Ahern what a tortuous, convoluted journey it would be until the day we received the final tape in April 2003. This was incidentally Richard Harris's recording of his own poem 'Christy Brown Came To Town' which had been provided for us by the BBC's *Parkinson* show. The Harris family had been extremely helpful in securing this, no doubt helped immeasurably by the fact that Richard Harris had written to us expressing his enthusiasm and, indeed, his sense of being 'honoured to take part'. He was particularly conscious of the fact that the project was for the benefit of the homeless in Ireland as he often ventured from his suite at the Savoy Hotel and mingled with London's homeless community on the nearby Embankment.

The journey certainly was tortuous, convoluted,

frustrating, time consuming and exasperating but this was infinitely more than compensated for by the myriad magical moments and the sheer joy of connecting, however briefly, with so many varied, talented and gifted individuals who embraced the idea with enthusiasm and generosity.

The recording process involved over 100 contributors providing a rich assortment of experiences too numerous to document in their entirety. My personal favourites include the delightful Miriam O'Callaghan recording in our studio, Westland, the poem *A Woman Untouched* by Frank McGuinness. This poem is a tribute to Miriam's late sister Anne who died so tragically young of cancer. I knew Anne who was beautiful in every sense of the word and this, indeed, was a moving and poignant moment.

There was the lovely sunny day in Dalkey when Judy and I enjoyed the infectious good humour of Maeve Binchy during the preamble to and recording of *Pangur Bán*. We enjoyed the passion and articulation of Bob Geldof in his hotel suite at Dublin's Westbury Hotel, the easy charm, presence and wonderful voice of Des Lynam, the unassuming Pierce Brosnan announcing himself to our startled receptionist at the record company with 'Brosnan, I'm working here today', the sheer professionalism of Gay Byrne, laughing uncontrollably with Jimmy Magee in the RTE studios, Bill Cullen offering his advice on 'How to become a millionaire before you're 30' to our young sound recordist Greg French who did such a brilliant job on all the recordings. There were so many more.

Graham Molloy, my eldest son, who has been another member of the core team worked with Bono, who recorded Brendan Kennelly's *God's Laughter*. Graham was impressed by the U2 man's attention to detail and his good natured enthusiasm for the project. He also worked with John Hume and found that uplifting. John's rendition of *Claudy* moved all of us. Also very moving was Sharon Corr's recording of *First Annual Report* written by her father, Gerry, as a tribute to her late mother.

I could recite so many instances that will provide golden memories when I dip into this volume in future years. There was a surreal moment when I found myself being given an impromptu but valuable golf lesson by Dermot Desmond in his stunning boardroom atop the IFSC building after he had recorded Thomas Davis's *My Land*. Meeting interesting and charming people like Milo O'Shea, Colin Farrell, Niall Quinn and Deirdre O'Kane and I might add Theo Dorgan made the whole project thoroughly enjoyable for me and hardly worthy of being called work.

Work is the key word which leads me to the long list of people without whom the project would have been impossible to complete. Right at the top of that list is Judy Cardiff who has been a veritable powerhouse. Judy, with her irresistible combination of charm, efficiency and unfailing good humour co-ordinated everything. She drove us all – arranging the recordings, obtaining the texts, liaising with Poetry Ireland, Focus Ireland and every individual contributor and many of the poets, organising photos, biogs, clearances and all the innumerable details required to complete each individual recording. It was a mammoth logistical task and she accomplished it beautifully despite the instances when we felt like giving up on specific individual contributions that for one reason or another were simply not happening.

I will try to list the names separately of the people who helped in various ways to bring this home and hope that I have not inadvertently left anyone out. There have been so many friends, colleagues and associates that I have blithely begged, cajoled and imposed upon but almost never have I found anything other than warm generosity and good will. Long time friends and colleagues Denis Desmond and John McColgan really put themselves out to help with Van Morrison and Gabriel Byrne respectively. Willie O'Reilly at Today FM put studios at our disposal. Alastair McGuckian and Ros and John Hubbard of Hubbard Casting could not have been more helpful. The wonderfully good natured Brendan Kennelly could not have been more accommodating as was the unassuming and infinitely resourceful Joe Woods of Poetry Ireland.

John Hughes and Barry Gaster have been supportive from day one. My friend, John Sheehan of

Sony Music, really went the extra mile and, indeed, was largely instrumental in bringing HarperCollins on board. Good friends like Nigel Duke, Tom Costello, Jeananne Crowley, Mike Murphy and Joe King, whom I shamelessly bored over dinner by talking about our project, were relentlessly enthusiastic and unstinting in their advice. My family led by my daughter, Nikki, even lifted the embargo on business talk over dinner which was when I really knew that I had them on side.

I have been handsomely rewarded by the contribution of this idea and seeing it through to fruition. It has given me a great sense of satisfaction and indeed all of the team share a sense of achievement. I am doubly gratified that Focus Ireland, so ably represented by the delightful Caroline Hickson, and its wonderful work to aid the homeless in Ireland will be helped considerably by the proceeds of this work.

BRIAN MOLLOY

Voices and Poetry of Ireland

READ BY BERTIE AHERN

The Mother

PADRAIC PEARSE

I do not grudge them: Lord, I do not grudge
My two strong sons that I have seen go out
To break their strength and die, they and a few,
In bloody protest for a glorious thing,
They shall be spoken of among their people,
The generations shall remember them,
And call them blessed;
But I will speak their names to my own heart
In the long nights;
The little names that were familiar once
Round my dead hearth.
Lord, thou art hard on mothers:
We suffer in their coming and their going;
And tho' I grudge them not, I weary, weary
Of the long sorrow – And yet I have my joy:
My sons were faithful, and they fought.

Bertie Ahern was elected Taoiseach (Leader of the Irish
Government) in 1997. He was re-elected Taoiseach in
2002. Born in Dublin in 1951, he was first elected to
Dail Eireann in 1977 and became leader of the Fianna
Fail Party in 1994. He was Dublin's Lord Mayor between
1986 and 1987 and has held various Ministries,
including Finance three times.

A Glass of Beer

JAMES STEPHENS

READ BY ROBERT BALLAGH

The lanky hank of a she in the inn over there
Nearly killed me for asking the loan of a glass of beer;
May the devil grip the whey-faced slut by the hair,
And beat bad manners out of her skin for a year.

That parboiled ape, with the toughest jaw you will see
On virtue's path, and a voice that would rasp the dead,
Came roaring and raging the minute she looked at me,
And threw me out of the house on the back of my head!

If I asked her master he'd give me a cask a day;
But she, with the beer at hand, not a gill would arrange!
May she marry a ghost and bear him a kitten, and may
The High King of Glory permit her to get the mange.

Robert Ballagh is one of Ireland's most distinguished artists
and designers. As a painter, his work is represented in
many important collections, including the National
Gallery of Ireland. He has designed stamps for the Irish
postal service and bank notes for the Central Bank of
Ireland. His striking stage designs, including *Riverdance*,
have enjoyed international acclaim.

The Mystery

AMERGIN

(TRANSLATED BY DOUGLAS HYDE)

READ BY PATRICK BERGIN

I am the wind which breathes upon the sea,
I am the wave of the ocean,
I am the murmur of the billows,
I am the ox of the seven combats,
I am the vulture upon the rocks,
I am a beam of the sun,
I am the fairest of plants,
I am a wild boar in valour,
I am a salmon in the water,
I am a lake in the plain,
I am a word of science,
I am the point of the lance of battle,
I am the God who created in the head the fire.
Who is it who throws light into the meeting on the mountain?

Who announces the ages of the moon?
Who teaches the place where couches the sun?
    (If not I)

Patrick Bergin was born and raised in Dublin. He has
appeared in myriad film and television productions,
including *Robin Hood* and *Patriot Games*, and co-starred
with Julia Roberts in the Hollywood hit film *Sleeping with
the Enemy*.

Pangur Bán

ANONYMOUS

TRANSLATED BY ROBIN FLOWER

READ BY MAEVE BINCHY

I and Pangur Bán, my cat,
’Tis a like task we are at;
Hunting mice is his delight,
Hunting words I sit all night.

Better far than praise of men
’Tis to sit with book and pen;
Pangur bears me no ill will,
He too plies his simple skill.

’Tis a merry thing to see
At our tasks how glad are we,
When at home we sit and find
Entertainment to our mind.

Oftentimes a mouse will stray
In the hero Pangur’s way;
Oftentimes my keen thought set
Takes a meaning in its net.

’Gainst the wall he sets his eye
Full and fierce and sharp and sly;
’Gainst the wall of knowledge I
All my little wisdom try.

When a mouse darts from its den,
O how glad is Pangur then!
O what gladness do I prove
When I solve the doubts I love!

So in peace our tasks we ply,
Pangur Bán, my cat and I;
In our hearts we find our bliss,
I have mine and he has his.

Practice every day has made
Pangur perfect in his trade;
I get wisdom day and night
Turning darkness into light.

Maeve Binchy was born in Co Dublin and was educated
at University College Dublin. Her first novel was published
in 1982 and was an instant success. Since then she
has written more than a dozen novels and short story
collections, each of them bestsellers. She is married to
the writer and broadcaster Gordon Snell.

Danny

J M SYNGE

READ BY CHARLIE BIRD

One night a score of Erris men,
A score I'm told and nine,
Said 'We'll get shut of Danny's
   noise
Of girls and widows dyin'.

'There's not his like from
   Binghamstown
To Boyle and Ballycroy,
At playing hell on decent girls,
At beating man and boy.

'He's left two pairs of female twins
Beyond in Killacreest,
And twice in Crossmolina fair
He's struck the parish priest.

'But we'll come round him in the
   night
A mile beyond the Mullet:
Ten will quench his bloody eyes,
And ten will choke his gullet.'

It wasn't long till Danny came,
From Bangor making way,
And he was damning moon and
   stars
And whistling grand and gay,

Till in a gap of hazel glen –
And not a hare in sight –
Out lepped the nine-and-twenty
   lads
Along his left and right.

Then Danny smashed the nose of
   Byrne,
He split the lips on three,
And bit across the right hand thumb
Of one Red Shawn Magee.

But seven tripped him up behind,
And seven kicked before,
And seven squeezed around his
   throat
Till Danny kicked no more.

Then some destroyed him with their
   heels,
Some tramped him in the mud,
Some stole his purse and timber
   pipe,
And some washed off his blood.

And when you're walking out the
   way
From Bangor to Belmullet,
You'll see a flat cross on a stone
Where men choked Danny's gullet.

Charlie Bird is the Chief News Correspondent for RTE where he has worked for almost twenty-five years. During that period he has covered many major domestic and international news stories. In 1998, along with his colleague George Lee, he was nominated Journalist of the Year for his work on various banking scandals.

Nuala

BRENDAN KENNELLY

READ BY TARA BLAZE

There's no shortage of sadness in the world,
The woman said, looking at Nuala, the child
Who was close to a grown girl now.
I remember Nuala, rampant and wild
In the village, banging at doors
Whenever she wished, running, then standing alone
With a wistful look in her eyes
As if she'd say something no-one
Could follow. The years passed. Her wild ways
Grew to be loved by the people,
Her presence helped many's the girl and boy
Suffering their own troubles. Her wistful gaze
Was a soft rain falling
On sadness, touching it with joy.

Tara Blaze is a singer-songwriter from Dublin whose
first lyrics feature on the album 'Wild Ocean'. This
album also includes such artists as The Corrs and The
Chieftains. Her first solo album will be launched in
2004.

Mirror in February

THOMAS KINSELLA

The day dawns with scent of must and rain,
Of opened soil, dark trees, dry bedroom air.
Under the fading lamp, half dressed – my brain
Idling on some compulsive fantasy –
I towel my shaven lip and stop, and stare,
Riveted by a dark exhausted eye,
A dry downturning mouth.

It seems again that it is time to learn,
In this untiring, crumbling place of growth
To which, for the time being, I return.
Now plainly in the mirror of my soul
I read that I have looked my last on youth
And little more; for they are not made whole
That reach the age of Christ

Below my window the awakening trees,
Hacked clean for better bearing, stand defaced
Suffering their brute necessities,
And how should the flesh not quail that span for span
Is mutilated more? In slow distaste
I fold my towel with what grace I can,
Not young and not renewable, but man.

READ BY LUKA BLOOM

Luka Bloom was born Barry Moore in 1955 in
Newbridge, Co Kildare. In 1987 he went to the US and
created 'Luka Bloom'. Since then he has enjoyed success
throughout the world with his songs, CDs and shows.

God's Laughter

BRENDAN KENNELLY

READ BY BONO

Bono is the lead singer of Irish rock group U2. U2
released their first album in 1980 and have since sold
over 100 million albums worldwide, winning 14
Grammys and six Brit Awards along the way. Bono lives
in Dublin with his wife and four children.

Someone had mercy on language
changed it into something else I can touch
I can touch
        grow to love, murmured Ace
as he heard the stranger talking of how
laughter comes from God.

Who, hearing words from his own mouth
and from others, can stop himself
laughing or freezing in terror

at sound bubbling up out of infinite
emptiness? Well, fill it with pride
and let vanity strut along for the ride.

When the ride peters out at the edge
of small daring, that other sound
opens.
        This is the sound of God's laughter,
like nothing on earth, it fills
earth from grave to mountain-top,
lingers there a while, then like a great
bird spreading its wings for home or somewhere
like home,
        heads out into silence,
gentle and endless, longing to understand

children, killers of children, killers. Mercy. Silence. Sound.
Mercy. Sound. Word. Sound. Change, there must be
change. There is. Say flesh. Say love. Say dust.
Say laughter. Who will call the fled bird back?
Stand. Kneel. Curse. Pray. Give us this day
our daily laughter. Let it show the way.
Thank God someone has mercy
on the words we find we must say.

A Little Boy in the Morning

FRANCIS LEDWIDGE

He will not come, and still I wait.
He whistles at another gate
Where angels listen. Ah I know
He will not come, yet if I go
How shall I know he did not pass
barefooted in the flowery grass?

The moon leans on one silver horn
Above the silhouettes of morn,
And from their nest-sills finches whistle
Or stooping pluck the downy thistle.
How is the morn so gay and fair
Without his whistling in its air?

The world is calling, I must go.
How shall I know he did not pass
Barefooted in the shining grass?

READ BY JOHN BOWMAN

John Bowman is a broadcaster and historian. He presents
current affairs and historical programmes for RTE. He is
author of *De Valera and the Ulster Question* and co-author
with Eimer Philbin Bowman of a book about their late
son, entitled *Jonathan.*

Four Voices Without an Instrument

MEDBH MCGUCKIAN

Another March month has come,
To raise the temperature of the
   world,
A self-opening, clear, in mourning,
Becoming light.

The northeast wind
Reads the quarters of the sky
Where the moon falls awake
Into its own mouth
Till day and night are equal.

There is no dust, no deluge.
The blue of the city has swollen
Or returned to itself
In its dark ship
The reverberating sea.

Even the light, I thought,
Like a bell in the air
Already out of tune
Through a slight snowfall,
Would never be allowed its
   brightness.

Yet since we have been a
   conversation,
The three-in-one sign
Of your stained-glass voice
Has become my chosen one,
A garden surrounded by other
   gardens,
Housing the seasons.

Though our lives may have
   overlapped,
The musicians that blew out their
   candles
And left the stage, one by one,
Now blow for me
A sunburst of winds
On their lowest strings;

So that not without wings,
When the mist vanishes,
The brightening, endangered earth
Is the year's first angel.

Paul Brady has been at the forefront of music in Ireland, both traditional and contemporary, for over thirty years. His songs have been recorded by artists worldwide, including Ronan Keating and Cher. He was recently awarded the Lifetime Achievement Award by the Irish Recorded Music Association.

Father and Son

F R HIGGINS

READ BY PIERCE BROSNAN

Only last week, walking the hushed
fields
Of our most lovely Meath, now
thinned by November,
I came to where the road from
Laracor leads
To the Boyne river - that seemed
more lake than river,
Stretched in uneasy light and stript
of reeds.

And walking longside an old weir
Of my people's, where nothing stirs
— only the shadowed
Leaden flight of a heron up the lean
air —
I went unmanly with grief, knowing
how my father,
Happy though captive in years,
walked last with me there.

Yes, happy in Meath with me for a
day
He walked, taking stock of herds
hid in their own breathing;
And naming colts, gusty as wind,
once steered by his hand,
Lightnings winked in the eyes that
were half shy in greeting
Old friends — the wild blades,
when he gallivanted the land.

For that proud, wayward man now
my heart breaks —
Breaks for that man whose mind
was a secret eyrie,
Whose kind hand was sole signet of
his race,
Who curbed me, scorned my green
ways, yet increasingly loved me
Till Death drew its grey blind down
his face.

And yet I am pleased that even my
reckless ways
Are living shades of his rich calms
and passions —
Witnesses for him and for those
faint namesakes
With whom now he is one, under
yew branches,
Yes, one in a graven silence no bird
breaks.

Pierce Brosnan is best known for his role as the current
James Bond. His work includes films such as *Dante's Peak*
and *The Thomas Crown Affair*, as well as the Bond
movies *Goldeneye, Tomorrow Never Dies, The World Is
Not Enough* and *Die Another Day*. Originally from Co
Meath, he now lives in California with his family.

A Christmas Childhood

PATRICK KAVANAGH

I

One side of the potato-pits was white with frost –
How wonderful that was, how wonderful!
And when we put our ears to the paling-post
The music that came out was magical.

The light between the ricks of hay and straw
Was a hole in Heaven's gable. An apple tree
With its December-glinting fruit we saw –
O you, Eve, were the world that tempted me

To eat the knowledge that grew in clay
And death the germ within it! Now and then
I can remember something of the gay
Garden that was childhood's. Again

The tracks of cattle to a drinking-place,
A green stone lying sideways in a ditch
Or any common sight the transfigured face
Of a beauty that the world did not touch.

II

My father played the melodeon
Outside at our gate;
There were stars in the morning east
And they danced to his music.

Across the wild bogs his melodeon called
To Lennons and Callans.
As I pulled on my trousers in a hurry
I knew some strange thing had happened.

READ BY VINCENT BROWNE

Vincent Browne is one of Ireland's best known print and broadcast journalists. His nightly radio programme for RTE, *Tonight with Vincent Browne*, is hugely popular and he writes a regular column in the *Irish Times*.

Outside in the cow-house my mother
Made the music of milking;
The light of her stable-lamp was a star
And the frost of Bethlehem made it twinkle.

A water-hen screeched in the bog,
Mass-going feet
Crunched the wafer-ice on the pot-holes,
Somebody wistfully twisted the bellows wheel.

My child poet picked out the letters
On the grey stone,
In silver the wonder of a Christmas townland,
The winking glitter of a frosty dawn.

Cassiopeia was over
Cassidy's hanging hill,
I looked and three whin bushes rode across
The horizon – the Three Wise Kings.

An old man passing said:
'Can't he make it talk' –
The melodeon. I hid in the doorway
And tightened the belt of my box-pleated coat.

I nicked six nicks on the door-post
With my penknife's big blade –
There was a little one for cutting tobacco.
And I was six Christmases of age.

My father played the melodeon,
My mother milked the cows,
And I had a prayer like a white rose pinned
On the Virgin Mary's blouse.

To L.L.

OSCAR WILDE

Could we dig up this long-buried treasure,
Were it worth the pleasure,
We never could learn love's song,
We are parted too long.

Could the passionate past that is fled
Call back its dead,
Could we live it all over again,
Were it worth the pain!

I remember we used to meet
By an ivied seat,
And you warbled each pretty word
With the air of a bird;

And your voice had a quaver in it,
Just like a linnet,
And shook, as the blackbird's throat
With its last big note;

And your eyes, they were green and grey
Like an April day,
But lit into amethyst
When I stooped and kissed;

And your mouth, it would never smile
For a long, long while,
Then it rippled all over with laughter
Five minutes after.

You were always afraid of a shower,
Just like a flower:
I remember you started and ran
When the rain began.

I remember I never could catch you,
For no one could match you,
You had wonderful, luminous, fleet
Little wings to your feet.

Gabriel Byrne was born in Dublin. His acting career began at Dublin's Focus Theatre and he has since starred in over 35 films, including *The Usual Suspects*, *Stigmata* and *End of Days*. He resides in New York.

I remember your hair – did I tie it?
For it always ran riot –
Like a tangled sunbeam of gold:
These things are old.

I remember so well the room,
And the lilac bloom
That beat at the dripping pane
In the warm June rain;

And the colour of your gown,
It was amber-brown,
And two yellow satin bows
From your shoulders rose.

And the handkerchief of French
  lace
Which you held to your face –
Had a small tear left a stain?
Or was it the rain?

On your hand as it waved adieu
There were veins of blue;
In your voice as it said good-bye
Was a petulant cry,

'You have only wasted your life.'
  (Ah, that was the knife!)
When I rushed through the garden
  gate
It was all too late.

Could we live it over again,
Were it worth the pain,
Could the passionate past that is
  fled
Call back its dead!

Well, if my heart must break,
Dear love, for your sake,
It will break in music, I know,
Poets' hearts break so.

But strange that I was not told
That the brain can hold
In a tiny ivory cell,
God's heaven and hell.

Mid-Term Break

SEAMUS HEANEY

I sat all morning in the college sick bay
Counting bells knelling classes to a close.
At two o'clock our neighbours drove me home.

In the porch I met my father crying –
He had always taken funerals in his stride –
And Big Jim Evans saying it was a hard blow.

The baby cooed and laughed and rocked the pram
When I came in, and I was embarrassed
By old men standing up to shake my hand

And tell me they were 'sorry for my trouble'.
Whispers informed strangers I was the eldest,
Away at school, as my mother held my hand

In hers and coughed out angry tearless sighs.
At ten o'clock the ambulance arrived
With the corpse, stanched and bandaged by the nurses.

Next morning I went up into the room. Snowdrops
And candles soothed the bedside; I saw him
For the first time in six weeks. Paler now,

Wearing a poppy bruise on his left temple,
He lay in the four-foot box as in his cot.
No gaudy scars, the bumper knocked him clear.

A four-foot box, a foot for every year.

Legendary broadcaster Gay Byrne was born in Dublin in 1934. *The Late Late Show,* of which he was host and executive producer, was Ireland's top-rating talk show for decades. He is married to the harpist and singer Kathleen Watkins and they have two daughters.

Liam Clancy is a founder member of the Clancy Brothers and Tommy Maken group. He was resident actor at Harvard's Poet Theater in 1957–58 and in 1960 co-produced Yeats's plays at New York's Poetry Center. He received an honorary doctorate from the University of Limerick in 2002, the same year as his first volume of memoirs, *The Mountain of the Women*, was published.

The Second Coming

W B YEATS

Turning and turning in the widening gyre
The falcon cannot hear the falconer;
Things fall apart; the centre cannot hold;
Mere anarchy is loosed upon the world,
The blood-dimmed tide is loosed, and everywhere
The ceremony of innocence is drowned;
The best lack all convictions, while the worst
Are full of passionate intensity.

Surely some revelation is at hand;
Surely the Second Coming is at hand.
The Second Coming! Hardly are those words out
When a vast image out of *Spiritus Mundi*
Troubles my sight: somewhere in sands of the desert
A shape with lion body and the head of a man,
A gaze blank and pitiless as the sun,
Is moving its slow thighs, while all about it
Reel shadows of the indignant desert birds.
The darkness drops again; but now I know
That twenty centuries of stony sleep
Were vexed to nightmare by a rocking cradle,
And what rough beast, its hour come round at last,
Slouches towards Bethlehem to be born?

The Friction of Feet in Time

MICHAEL COADY

READ BY PADDY COLE

Once upon those nights
with Joe Carroll on trumpet
Jack Doherty on bass
and my mother on piano

with myself at seventeen on
    trombone
and Davy Breen the hunchback
    keeping time
on bass drum and brushed calfskin.

Once upon some little hall located
along byroads difficult to find

before the broken lid
is closed on the piano
and the band packed for the road

before the person with the key
turns out the lights
on dusty creak and scented
sigh of absence

my uncle Peter lays aside the sax to
    sing
          Goodnight sweetheart
          Till we meet tomorrow

over heads of men and women
moving clockwise in their holding
of each other and the moment
and the music that embraced them.

Once upon those nights
if you stood outside the hall
you could hear in the dark

the shuffling unanimity
of feet in time

like a grounded being
moving underneath the music
in a relentless drag and slide –

shoo   shoo   shoo-sha   shoo
shoo   shoo   shoo-sha   shoo.

That against the gravity of darkness
over and around a little hall
past byroads difficult to find

once upon those nights of
shoo   shoo   shoo-sha   shoo
shoo   shoo   shoo-sha   shoo.
once   once   once   upon
once   once   once   upon
shoo   shoo   shoo-sha   shoo

Paddy Cole has been a household name in Ireland for many years. A hugely popular musician and entertainer, he has hosted his own television and radio shows. Five years in a Las Vegas show led to tours of the US and Canada, and all over the world.

Never Give All the Heart

W B YEATS

Never give all the heart, for love
Will hardly seem worth thinking of
To passionate women if it seem
Certain, and they never dream
That it fades out from kiss to kiss;
For everything that's lovely is
But a brief, dreamy, kind delight.
O never give the heart outright,
For they, for all smooth lips can say,
Have given their hearts up to the play.
And who could play it well enough
If deaf and dumb and blind with love?
He that made this knows all the cost,
For he gave all his heart and lost.

READ BY ANDREA CORR

Andrea Corr is the lead singer of the multi-million album
selling band The Corrs. She has appeared in the films
The Commitments, *Evita* and *The Boys from County Clare*.

First Annual Report

GERRY CORR

READ BY SHARON CORR

A year on, my love,
A year since we parted,
You to the prayer-wrapped
    unknown,
Me to a cell called freedom

In your place I have memory,
A stingy usurper
Dispensing crumbs
From the banquet of your table

Like a donkey in Omeath
Kicking my pride
And your laughter
Animating the Mournes

Or champagne Saturday
When we whooped and danced
To new celestial arrivals
On our cherished firmament,

Your light is on dim now, my love,
Yet blinding flashes of you
Startle me awake
From the barren limbo of dreams,

You'll be pleased God is back.
He left when you died.
Went a.w.o.l.
Like He'd been found out
Not having the answers
And permitting instead a soothing
    indulgence:
Why hast Thou forsaken me

Yet there again, my dear,
I must allow for pre-occupation
With glamorous new arrival,
Introductions all round,
Glasses raised and all that,
Your's a spritzer, my love?

That's about it for now, my dear,
Except to say the blubbering is
    ceased
And sorrow's sickly syrup of self
Expunged from the menu

Well…in hope and in prayer, that is,

My love

Sharon Corr plays violin in The Corrs. The Corrs have
sold 30 million records and have won awards globally,
together with two Grammy nominations for their 'In Blue'
album. Sharon reads her father's poem.

The Man from God Knows Where

FLORENCE WILSON

Into our townlan', on a night of
  snow,
Rode a man from God-knows-
  where;
None of us bade him stay or go,
Nor deemed him friend, nor
  damned him foe,
But we stabled his big roan mare:
For in our townlan' we're decent
  folk
And if he didn't speak, why none of
  us spoke,
And we sat till the fire burned low.

We're a civil sort in our wee place,
So we made the circle wide
Round Andy Lemon's cheerful
  blaze,
And wished the man his length of
  days,
And a good end to his ride.
He smiled in under his slouchy hat –
Says he: 'There's a bit of a joke in
  that,
For we ride different ways.'
The whiles we smoked we watched
  him stare

from his seat fornenst the glow,
I nudged Joe Moore; 'You wouldn't
  dare
To ask him, who he's for meeting
  there,
And how far he has to go.'
But Joe wouldn't dare, nor Willy
  Scott
And he took no drink – neither cold
  nor hot –
this Man from God-knows-where.

It was closin' time, an' late forbye,
When us ones braved the air –
I never saw worse (may I live or die)
Then the sleet that night, an' I says,
  says I:
'You'll find he's for stopping there.'
But at screek o' day, through the
  gable pane
I watched him spur in the peltin'
  rain
And I juked from his rovin' eye.

Well t'was gettin' on past the heat o'
    the year
When I rode to Newtown Fair:
I sold as I could the dealers were
    near –
Only three pounds eight for the
    Innish steer,
(An' nothin' at all for the mare!)
I met M'Kee in the throng o' the
    street,
Says he: 'The grass has grown
    under our feet
Since they hanged young Warwick
    here.

And he told me that Boney had
    promised help
To a man in Dublin town.
Says he: 'If ye've laid the pike on
    the shelf
Ye'd better go home hot-fut by yer-
    self,
An' once more take it down.'
So by Comber road I trotted the
    grey
And never cut corn until Killyleagh
Stood plain on the risin' groun'.

For a wheen o' days we sat waitin'
    the word
To rise and go at it like men.
But no French ships sailed into
    Cloughey Bay,
And we heard the black news on a
    harvest day
That the cause was lost again;
and Joey and me, and Wully Boy
    Scott,
We agreed to ourselves we'd as lief
    as not
Ha' been found in the thick o' the
    slain.

By Downpatrick gaol I was bound
    to fare
On a day I'll remember, feth,
For when I came to the prison
    square
The people were waitin' in hun-
    dreds there,
An' you wouldn't hear stir nor
    breath!
For the sodgers were standin', grim
    an' tall
Round a scaffold built there for-
    nenst the wall.
An' a man stepped out for death!

I was brave an' near to the edge of
    the throng,
Yet I knowed that face again.
An' I knowed the set, an' I knowed
    the walk
An' the sound of his strange up-
    country talk,
For he spoke out right an' plain.
Then he bowed his head to the
    swinging rope,
Whiles I said 'Please God' to his
    dying hope
And 'Amen' to his dying prayer,
That the Wrong would cease and
    the Right prevail,
For the man that they hanged at
    Downpatrick gaol
was The Man from GOD-
    KNOWS-WHERE.

The Bells of Shandon

FRANCIS SYLVESTER
MAHONY

READ BY JOHN CREEDON

John Creedon is a native of Cork City and a broadcaster on radio and television. He co-produces and presents the *John Creedon Show* for RTE, has toured Ireland's stand-up comedy circuit, and regularly hosted national award ceremonies and concerts.

With deep affection and recollection
 I often think of the Shandon bells,
Whose sounds so wild would, in days of childhood,
 Fling round my cradle their magic spells.
On this I ponder, where'er I wander,
 And thus grow fonder, sweet Cork, of thee;
  With thy bells of Shandon,
  That sound so grand on
The pleasant waters of the river Lee.

I have heard bells chiming full many a clime in,
 Tolling sublime in cathedral shrine;
While at a glib rate brass tongues would vibrate,
 But all their music spoke nought to thine;
For memory dwelling on each proud swelling
 Of thy belfry knelling its bold notes free,
  Made the bells of Shandon
  Sound far more grand on
The pleasant waters of the river Lee.

I have heard bells tolling 'old Adrian's mole' in,
 Their thunder rolling from the Vatican,
With cymbals glorious, swinging uproarious
 In the gorgeous turrets of Notre Dame;
But thy sounds were sweeter than the dome of Peter
 Flings o'er the Tiber, pealing solemnly.
  Oh! the bells of Shandon
  Sound far more grand on
The pleasant waters of the river Lee.

There's a bell in Moscow, while on tower and Kiosko
 In St Sophia the Turkman gets,
And loud in air calls men to prayer
 From the tapering summit of tall minarets.
Such empty phantom I freely grant 'em,
 But there's an anthem more dear to me:
  'Tis the bells of Shandon,
  That sound so grand on
The pleasant waters of the river Lee.

The Fisherman

W B YEATS

READ BY ANTHONY CRONIN

Although I can see him still,
The freckled man who goes
To a grey place on a hill
In grey Connemara clothes
At dawn to cast his flies,
It's long since I began
To call up to the eyes
This wise and simple man.
All day I'd looked in the face
What I had hoped 'twould be
To write for my own race
And the reality;
The living men that I hate,
The dead man that I loved,
The craven man in his seat,
The insolent unreproved,
And no knave brought to book
Who has won a drunken cheer,
The witty man and his joke
Aimed at the commonest ear,
The clever man who cries
The catch-cries of the clown,
The beating down of the wise
And great Art beaten down.

Maybe a twelvemonth since
Suddenly I began,
In scorn of this audience,
Imagining a man
And his sun-freckled face,
And grey Connemara cloth,
Climbing up to a place
Where stone is dark under froth,
And the down turn of his wrist
When the flies drop in the stream:
A man who does not exist,
A man who is but a dream;
And cried, 'Before I am old
I shall have written him one
Poem maybe as cold
And passionate as the dawn.'

Born in 1928 in Co Wexford, Anthony Cronin is a poet, novelist, critic and biographer. His novels include *Life of Riley* and *Identity Papers*. He has also published a biography of Flann O'Brien, *No Laughing Matter*, and a major biography of Samuel Beckett, *The Last Modernist*.

An Old Woman of the Roads

PADRAIC COLUM

O, to have a little house!
To own the hearth and stool and all!
The heaped up sods against the fire,
The pile of turf against the wall!

To have a clock with weights and
    chains
And pendulum swinging up and
    down!
A dresser filled with shining delph,
Speckled and white and blue and
    brown!

I could be busy all the day
Clearing and sweeping hearth and
    floor,
And fixing on their shelf again
My white and blue and speckled
    store!

I could be quiet there at night
Beside the fire and by myself,
Sure of a bed and loth to leave
The ticking clock and the shining
    delph!

Och! But I'm weary of mist and
    dark,
And roads where there's never a
    house nor bush,
And tired I am of bog and road,
And the crying wind and the
    lonesome hush!

And I am praying to God on high,
And I am praying Him night and
    day,
For a little house – a house of my
    own –
Out of the wind's and the rain's
    way.

Jeananne Crowley began her acting career in Dublin before joining the National Theatre in London. She wrote a documentary series, *Crown and Shamrock*, on the history of the Anglo-Irish for Channel 4 and played the title role in the mini-series *The Real Charlotte*. Jeananne currently lives between Cleggan, Co Galway and Dublin.

Bill Cullen is chairman of Renault Ireland and author of the bestselling novel *It's A Long Way From Penny Apples*. Born in 1942 in Dublin, he is now a director of the Irish Youth Foundation and resides in Co Kildare.

Shades of Ranelagh

MACDARA WOODS

As I came in from Drowned Lake Mountain
starved of money and dry to the bone, when
many long burned out years ago I was
caught good & proper on a nail spike streetscape,
another exploded sixties myth I was
caught good & proper on a judges ruling
and my schooldays wheeled up Ranelagh Road.
As usual indiscipline I found me walking
before and after all along Vergemount
where the Muckross girls drift by like clouds.
Is original sin still alive and well
on the shaded paths of the Dodder?
Does the fashion parade throw a daily shape
to the bridge and Portobello,
does everything stop by the Grand Canal
including the four ten bus to Yuma?
Are the celluloid cowboys up in the Sandford
still yodeling the blues in pure valerian,
taking tokes and pulling strokes
on the high chapparal of the fire escape
where Homer nods to Rowdy Yates?
As I sail in from Drowned Lake Mountain
On a nineteen forties turf-boat order
I sight my boat on the filled-in harbour
and dance my jigs without embargo,
by the Grand Canal where all things stop
my ballast is sticks of selskar rock.

for Niall

The Christmas Rose

C DAY LEWIS

What is the flower that blooms each year
In flowerless days,
Making a little blaze
On the bleak earth, giving my heart some cheer?

    Harsh the sky and hard the ground
    When the Christmas rose is found.
    Look! its white star, low on earth,
    Rays a vision of rebirth.

Who is the child that's born each year –
His bedding, straw:
His grace, enough to thaw
My wintering life, and melt a world's despair?

    Harsh the sky and hard the earth
    When the Christmas child comes forth.
    Look, around a stable throne
    Beasts and wise men are at one.

What men are we that, year on year
We Herod-wise
In our cold wits devise
A death of innocents, a rule of fear?

    Hushed your earth, full-starred your sky
    For a new nativity:
    Be born in us, relieve our plight,
    Christmas child, you rose of light!

Ian Dempsey hosts the popular *Breakfast Show on* Today
FM. Born in 1961 in Dublin, and a graduate of
Belvedere College, he quickly established himself as a
prominent figure in Irish broadcasting after joining RTE
in 1980. He lives in Sutton, Co Dublin with his wife
and family.

Duffy's Circus

PAUL MULDOON

Once Duffy's Circus had shaken out its tent
In the big field near the Moy
God may as well have left Ireland
And gone up a tree. My father had said so.

There was no such thing as the five-legged calf,
The God of creation
Was the God of Love.
My father chose to share such Nuts of Wisdom.

Yet across the Alps of each other the elephants
Trooped. Nor did it matter
When Wild Bill's Rain Dance
Fell flat. Some clown emptied a bucket of stars

Over the swankiest part of the crowd.
I had lost my father in the rush and slipped
Out the back. Now I heard
For the first time that long-drawn-out cry.

It came from somewhere beyond the corral.
A dwarf on stilts. Another dwarf.
I sidled past some trucks. From under a freighter
I watched a man sawing a woman in half.

My Land

THOMAS DAVIS

She is a rich and rare land,
Oh she's a fresh and fair land;
She is a dear and rare land,
This native land of mine.

No men than hers are braver,
Her women's hearts ne'er waver;
I'd freely die to save her,
And think my lot divine.

She's not a dull or cold land,
No, she's a warm and bold land,
Oh, she's a true and old land,
This native land of mine.

Could beauty ever guard her,
And virtue still reward her,
No foe would cross her border –
No friend within it pine.

Oh, she's a fresh and fair land,
Oh, she's a true and rare land;
Yes she's a rare and fair land,
This native land of mine.

Dermot Desmond is Chairman of International Investment
and Underwriting Limited which he founded in 1995
and which has investments in a variety of businesses
including London City Airport, the Sandy Lane Hotel in
Barbados and Celtic Football Club.

Winter Birds

MOYA CANNON

READ BY MOYA DOHERTY

I have frequently seen, with my own eyes, more than a thousand of these
small birds hanging down on the sea-shore from one piece of timber,
enclosed in their shells and already formed.
– Giraldus Cambrensis, *Topographia Hiberniae*

From the cliffs of Northern Greenland
the black-breasted geese come down
to graze on the wind-bitten sedges of Inis Cé.
They land in October, exhausted,
bringing with them their almost-grown young.

No one on these shores could ever find their nests,
so in early times it was concluded
that they had been hatched from the pupa-shaped goose barnacle.
Being fish, they could be eaten on Friday.

In April they gather, restless, broody,
fatted on the scant new grasses of a continent's margin,
ready to leave for breeding grounds in Greenland's tundra.

Watching that nervous strut and clamour –
a tuning orchestra raucous
before the signal
to rise on the wind
in a harmony
old as hunger –
the name grips somewhere else,
my father's talk of 'winter-birds' in his class
in South Donegal,
the name his schoolmaster had given
to big boys
who sat in the back seats,
back from the Lagan or Scotland,
already seasoned,
their migratory patterns set.

In 1994, as Executive Producer of the Eurovision Song
Contest for RTE, Moya Doherty produced *Riverdance* as
the interval entertainment. Moya went on to produce
Riverdance The Show, now an acclaimed theatrical
spectacle worldwide. In 1997 she was voted Veuve
Clicquot Business Woman of the Year and received the
Ernst and Young Entrepreneur of the Year Award in 1999.
In 2002 Moya received an Honorary Doctorate of Letters
from the University of Ulster and was bestowed with an
Honorary Doctorate of Letters by the National University
of Ireland in 2003.

Death of an Irishwoman

MICHAEL HARTNETT

Ignorant, in the sense
she ate monotonous food
and thought the world was flat,
and pagan, in the sense
she knew the things that moved
at night were neither dogs nor cats
but púcas and darkfaced men,
she nevertheless had fierce pride.
But sentenced in the end
to eat thin diminishing porridge
in a stone-cold kitchen
she clenched her brittle hands
around a world
she could not understand.
I loved her from the day she died.
She was a summer dance at the crossroads.
She was a card game where a nose was broken.
She was a song that nobody sings.
She was a house ransacked by soldiers.
She was a language seldom spoken.
She was a child's purse, full of useless things.

Theo Dorgan is a poet, editor, documentary scriptwriter
and broadcaster. Born in Cork in 1953 he has published
a number of collections of poetry including *The Ordinary
House of Love, Rosa Mundi* and *Sappho's Daughter*. He
lives in Baldoyle in North Dublin.

Nude

NUALA NÍ DHOMHNAILL

TRANSLATED BY PAUL MULDOON

READ BY ANNE DOYLE

The long and the short
of it is I'd rather see you nude –
your silk shirt
and natty

tie, the brolly under your oxter
in case of a rainy day,
the three-piece seersucker
suit that's so incredibly trendy,

your snazzy loafers
and, la-di-da,
a pair of gloves
made from the skin of a doe,

then, to top it all, a crombie hat
set at a rak-
ish angle – none of these add
up to more than icing on the cake.

For, unbeknownst to the rest
of the world, behind the outward
show lies a body unsurpassed
for beauty, without so much as a
    wart

or blemish, but the brill-
iant slink of a wild animal, a dream-
cat, say, on the prowl,
leaving murder and mayhem

in its wake. Your broad, sinewy
shoulders and your flank
smooth as the snow
on a snow-bank.

Your back, your slender waist,
and, of course,
the root that is the very seat
of pleasure, the pleasure-source.

Your skin so dark, my beloved,
and soft
as silk with a hint of velvet
in its weft,

smelling as it does of meadowsweet
or 'watermead'
that has the power, or so it's said,
to drive men and women mad.

For that reason alone, if for no other,
when you come with me to the
    dance tonight
(though, as you know, I'd much
    prefer
to see you nude)

it would be best
for you to pull on your pants and
    vest
rather than send
half the women of Ireland totally
    round the bend.

Anne Doyle was born in Ferns, Co Wexford. She is the main presenter on RTE's flagship nightly news programme *The 9 o'clock News*. A graduate of University College Dublin, she also presents *Crimeline*.

Pity the Islanders, Lucht an Oileáin

DAVID QUIN

READ BY DANNY DOYLE

For they dwelt on a rock in the sea and not in a shining metropolis
and lived off the pick of the strand, the hunt of the hill, the fish in the sea
the wool off the sheep, and packets full of dollars; for they ate black pudding,

drank sleadaí squeezed from seaweed, treated themselves on Good Fridays
to tit-bits from the shore, and thought a man rich if he possessed two cows;
for they stuffed their pillows with puffins' feathers, and the sea roared.

In their right ear and the north wind moaned in their left; for they were full
of sunlight and mist, wind and stone, rain and rock, but the Atlantic ocean
would not pay them a regular salary; and they did not fret about tumble
   driers

or grouse about the menu, for the wind would not let them strut, the
rain made them meek and the waves kept them low; for they feared
   vain-glory
and the evil eye, chewed bits of seaweed and prayed to the mother of God;

for their enemies were bailiffs, big fat trawlers, mainland shopkeepers
and crows after hens; for they made nothing fit for museum or art gallery
and uttered proverbs that came up from Cro Magnon man; for they lived

before Descartes, Newton, Freud, de Sade and Marx, invented no novel
   machine
or vice, and never discovered the multiple orgasm; for they lacked ambition,
built into the earth not the sky, and did not rob and plunder or scatter

corpses in their wake; for they lived before the age of trivia
and never made it to the age of anxiety, and did not suffer ennui because
there was turf to be cut; for they did not rush into the future,

leaving their hearts behind them, because they had no future.
Praise the islanders, lucht an Oileáin, for they were a fair people
who pelted the stranger with blessings and the bailiffs with volleys of stones;

Dublin musician and singer Danny Doyle was one of the leading voices in the Irish folk song revival of the 1960s. His number one hits include *Step it Out Mary, The Mucky Kid, Whiskey on a Sunday* and *The Rare Ould Times*. He now resides in Virginia.

for they were a gentle people, who twisted puffins' necks, patted babies'
    heads
and split the skulls of seals; for they were like the children of one mother
    with twenty
steps between each house; for they were quiet people, who never

stopped talking, full of malice and affection, whose delights were tea
and tobacco, a big ship on the waves, a donkey on the loose, a battle
of tongues, a boatful of rabbits, a dance, a story, a song in the dead of night;

for they were as mournful as wet sheep and as bright as gannets;
were pagans who trusted in God, rubbed seal oil on their wounds,
welcomed wrecks but prayed for the corpses, and loved to fill their bellies

with the breeze that flows from the west; for they broke their backs with
    loads of fish and sand, turf and lobsters, and leant on walls to bask in the
    sun;
for their stage was not the city, nation or world, but the village, the island
    and the
neighbouring parishes, which are about the right size for a human being.

When they strolled beneath the Milky Way their laughter did not pollute the
night, for they kept their boats high on the waves and their roofs low to the
    ground
and were grateful for seals when God withheld pigs.

Ode

ARTHUR O'SHAUGHNESSY

We are the music-makers,
And we are the dreamers of dreams,
Wandering by lone sea-breakers,
And sitting by desolate streams;
World-losers and world-forsakers,
On whom the pale moon gleams:
Yet we are the movers and shakers
Of the world for ever, it seems.

With wonderful deathless ditties
We build up the world's great cities,
And out of a fabulous story
We fashion an empire's glory:
One man with a dream, at pleasure,
Shall go forth and conquer a crown;
And three with a new song's measure
Can trample an empire down.

We, in the ages lying
In the buried past of the earth,
Built Nineveh with our sighing,
And Babel itself with our mirth;
And o'erthrew them with prophesying
To the old of the new world's worth;
For each age is a dream that is dying,
Or one that is coming to birth.

Someone

DENNIS O'DRISCOLL

someone is dressing up for death today, a change of skirt or tie
eating a final feast of buttered sliced pan, tea
scarcely having noticed the erection that was his last
shaving his face to marble for the icy laying out
spraying with deodorant her coarse armpit grass
someone today is leaving home on business
saluting, terminally, the neighbours who will join in the cortege
someone is trimming his nails for the last time, a precious moment
someone's thighs will not be streaked with elastic in the future
someone is putting out milkbottles for a day that will not come
someone's fresh breath is about to be taken clean away
someone is writing a cheque that will be marked 'drawer deceased'
someone is circling posthumous dates on a calendar
someone is listening to an irrelevant weather forecast
someone is making rash promises to friends
someone's coffin is being sanded, laminated, shined
who feels this morning quite as well as ever
someone if asked would find nothing remarkable in today's date
perfume and goodbyes her final will and testament
someone today is seeing the world for the last time
as innocently as he had seen it first

Joe Duffy presents RTE's *Liveline*, a popular phone-in
show. Born in 1956, Joe started out as a producer
and later became a reporter on *The Gay Byrne Show*.
This led to him presenting several programmes,
including the media programme *Soundbyte*.

To My Daughter Betty, The Gift Of God

THOMAS KETTLE

In wiser days, my darling rosebud, blown
To beauty proud as was your mother's prime,
In that desired, delayed, incredible time,
You'll ask why I abandoned you, my own,
And the dear heart that was your baby throne,
To dice with death. And oh! they'll give you rhyme
And reason: some will call the thing sublime,
And some decry it in a knowing tone.
So here, while the mad guns curse overhead,
And tired men sigh with mud for couch and floor,
Know that we fools, now with the foolish dead,
Died not for flag, nor King, nor Emperor,
But for a dream, born in a herdsman's shed,
And for the secret Scripture of the poor.

Myles Dungan is a broadcaster and author and currently presents the RTE programme *Rattlebag*. His writing credits include *Distant Drums: Irish Soldiers in Foreign Armies*, *Irish Voices from the Great War* and *They Shall Grow Not Old: The Irish in the Great War* and two plays – *Mansfield Park* and *The Jealous Wall*.

Dublin-born Eamon Dunphy represented Ireland 23 times as a professional footballer between 1960 and 1977. His first book, *Only a Game,* was published in 1976. He has written three other books – all biographies – his subjects being U2, Sir Matt Busby and Roy Keane, the latter of which was hugely successful as well as controversial. Eamon is now a broadcast journalist and presenter.

from *The Paddiad*

or The Devil as a Patron of Irish Letters

PATRICK KAVANAGH

…About the devil's dark intentions
There are some serious misconceptions:
The devil is supposed to be
A nasty man entirely,
Horned and hoofed and fearful gory –
That's his own invented story.

The truth in fact is the reverse
He does not know a single curse;
His forte's praise for what is dead,
Pegasus's Munnings bred.
Far and near he screws his eyes
In search of what will never rise,
Souls that are fusty, safe and dim,
These are the geniuses of the land to him.

Most generous-tempered of the gods
He listens to the vilest odes,
Aye, and not just idle praise!
For these the devil highly pays.
And the crowds for culture cheer and cheer:
'A modern Medici is here,
Never more can it be said
That Irish poets are not fed'
The boys go wild and toast the Joker
The master of the mediocre.

The Lovers

ANTHONY CRONIN

I went for a walk one evening
Through the streets of the city wide.
There were couples laughing and
    talking
And kissing on every side;

And I knew that for some that
    evening
In the city's golden haze
Would glow as a remembrance
Through other, different days;

That some of them would be loving
Through times which would seem
    without end,
Passionate, gentle, caring,
Friend to sexual friend.

And I laughed with the happy cou-
    ples,
Lost in a fond embrace,
Till I saw some in the future
Stand in another place,

Saw them glare at each other in
    anger
And rend each other with words
Like the claws of cruel leopards
Or the beaks of terrible birds;

Saw a time which would come for
    many
When, wounded and full of spite,
They would even rue the loving
Of this lovely city night.

And I prayed to Aphrodite,
That she might ease the pain
Which would flow from the bitter
    quarrels
Of parting, if parting came;

That the love which she now gave
    them
Might still somehow outlast
The lies and the resentments,
The twisting of the past;

And asked that she might spare
    them
As they tore themselves apart,
The fearful loss of fealty,
The freezing of the heart.

But as I walked up Dame Street
On my way home again,
I knew time holds us hostage
And that time brings us pain;

And thought at the chimes of Christ
    Church
Of the ever-flowing stream,
Bearing us into the future
As into another dream.

Paul Durcan was born in Dublin in 1944 and studied at University College Cork. His first book, *Endsville* (with Brian Lynch), was published in 1967, and has been followed by 17 others. In 1974 he won the Patrick Kavanagh Award and in1990 the Whitbread Poetry Award. He lives in Dublin.

July in Bettystown

GERARD FANNING

When the linen flaps open
With its east coast view of the
Mournes,
And Ian Fleming novelettes
Hide in a pile of fragrant clothes,

There is always the sea –
That reeling silence on a line,
And the clay like ground tarragon,
With its stench of burnished brine.

And always the hint of fire
The thatch in its myriad parts,
And the air full of black-tailed grass
That some times has red hearts.

Dave Fanning began his broadcasting career in 1979
with the fledgling radio station 2FM. He presents two
television programmes – *The Last Broadcast* and a film
review programme, *What Movie?*. He also presents
Music Express which is shown in 45 countries. Dave
is also film critic with the *Sunday World*. He lives in
Blackrock, Co Dublin with his wife, Ursula, and three
children.

Dublin Made Me

DONAGH MACDONAGH

Dublin made me and no little town
With the country closing in on its streets
The cattle walking proudly on its pavements
The jobbers, the gombeenmen and the cheats

Devouring the fair-day between them
A public-house to half a hundred men
And the teacher, the solicitor and the bank-clerk
In the hotel bar drinking for ten.

Dublin made me, not the secret poteen still
The raw and hungry hills of the West
The lean road flung over profitless bog
Where only a snipe could nest.

Where the sea takes its tithe of every boat.
Bawneen and currach have no allegiance of mine,
Nor the cute self-deceiving talkers of the South
Who look to the East for a sign.

The soft and dreary midlands with their tame canals
Wallow between sea and sea, remote from adventure,
And Northward a far and fortified province
Crouches under the lash of arid censure.

I disclaim all fertile meadows, all tilled land
The evil that grows from it and the good,
But the Dublin of old statutes, this arrogant city,
Stirs proudly and secretly in my blood.

Night Feed

EAVAN BOLAND

READ BY MARIAN FINUCANE

This is dawn
Believe me
This is your season, little daughter.
The moment daisies open,
The hour mercurial rainwater
Makes a mirror for sparrows.
It's time we drowned our sorrows.

I tiptoe in.
I lift you up
Wriggling
In your rosy, zipped sleeper.
Yes, this is the hour
For the early bird and me
When finder is keeper.

I crook the bottle.
How you suckle!
This is the best I can be,
Housewife
To this nursery
Where you hold on,
Dear life.

A silt of milk.
The last suck
And now your eyes are open,
Birth-coloured and offended.
Earth wakes.
You go back to sleep.
The feed is ended.

Worms turn.
Stars go in.
Even the moon is losing face.
Poplars stilt for dawn
And we begin
The long fall from grace.
I tuck you in.

Marian Finucane was born in Dublin and educated at
Scoil Chaitriona and the DIT. School of Architecture. She
joined RTE in 1974 as an announcer and currently pres-
ents the *Marian Finucane Show* on morning radio. Over
the course of her career she has been honoured with
broadcasting awards including Entertainer of the Year
Award and Woman of the Year Award.

Biddy Mulligan, The Pride of the Coombe

SEAMUS KAVANAGH

READ BY BRENDA FRICKER

I'm a buxom fine widow, I live in a
   spot,
In Dublin they call it the Coombe;
My shops and my stalls are laid out
   on the street,
And my palace consists of one room.
I sell apples and oranges, nuts and
   split peas,
Bananas and sugar-stick sweet,
On Saturday night I sell second-
   hand clothes
From the floor of my stall on the
   street.

You may travel from Clare
To the County Kildare,
From Francis Street on to Macroom,
But where would you see
A fine widow like me?
Biddy Mulligan, the pride of the Coombe.

I sell fish on a Friday, spread out on
   a board
The finest you'd find in the sae,
But the best is my herrings, fine
   Dublin Bay herrings,
There's herrings for dinner today.
I have a son Mick, and he's great on
   the flute
He plays in the Longford Street Band,
It would do your heart good to see
   him march out,
On a Sunday for Dollymount
   strand.

You may travel from Clare
To the County Kildare,
From Francis Street on to Macroom,
But where would you see
A fine widow like me?
Biddy Mulligan, the pride of the Coombe.

In the Park on a Sunday, I make
   quite a dash,
The neighbours look on with surprise,
With my Aberdeen shawlie thrown
   over my head,
I dazzle the sight of their eyes.
At Patrick Street corner for sixty-
   four years,
I've stood and no one can deny,
That while I stood there, no person
   could dare
To say black was the white of my
   eye.

You may travel from Clare
To the County Kildare,
From Francis Street on to Macroom,
But where would you see
A fine widow like me?
Biddy Mulligan, the pride of the Coombe.

Brenda Fricker was born in Dublin in 1945. In 1989 she won a Best Supporting Actress Oscar for her role in *My Left Foot*. She now works in films, television and theatre in Ireland, Great Britain and the United States.

from *The Ballad of Reading Gaol*

OSCAR WILDE

READ BY GAVIN FRIDAY

Gavin Friday was born in Dublin in 1959. He is
a singer, composer, performer and painter. He is
the founder member of the legendary avant-garde
punk group The Virgin Prunes.

...He did not wear his scarlet coat,
For blood and wine are red,
And blood and wine were on his
    hands
When they found him with the
    dead,
The poor dead woman whom he
    loved,
And murdered in her bed.

He walked amongst the Trial Men
In a suit of shabby grey;
A cricket cap was on his head,
And his step seemed light and gay;
But I never saw a man who looked
So wistfully at the day.

I never saw a man who looked
With such a wistful eye
Upon that little tent of blue
Which prisoners call the sky,
And at every drifting cloud that
    went
With sails of silver by.

I walked with other souls in pain,
Within another ring,
And was wondering if the man had
    done
A great or little thing,
When a voice behind me whispered
    low,
'That fellow's got to swing.'

Dear Christ! the very prison walls
Suddenly seemed to reel,
And the sky above my head became
Like a casque of scorching steel;

And, though I was a soul in pain,
My pain I could not feel.

I only knew what hunted thought
Quickened his step, and why
He looked upon the garish day
With such a wistful eye;
The man had killed the thing he
    loved,
And so he had to die.

Yet each man kills the thing he
    loves,
By each let this be heard,
Some do it with a bitter look,
Some with a flattering word,
The coward does it with a kiss,
The brave man with a sword!

Some kill their love when they are
    young,
And some when they are old;
Some strangle with the hands of
    Lust,
Some with the hands of Gold:
The kindest use a knife, because
The dead so soon grow cold.

Some love too little, some too long,
Some sell, and others buy;
Some do the deed with many tears,
And some without a sigh:
For each man kills the thing he
    loves,
Yet each man does not die.

READ BY SIR JAMES GALWAY

Sir James Galway was born in Belfast. He is regarded as both a supreme interpreter of the classical flute repertoire and a consummate entertainer. Through his extensive touring, over fifty best-selling RCA Victor albums, and his frequent television appearances, Sir James has endeared himself to millions worldwide.

The Rain Stick

SEAMUS HEANEY

Up-end the rain stick and what happens next
Is a music that you never would have known
To listen for. In a cactus stalk

Downpour, sluice-rush, spillage and backwash
Come flowing through. You stand there like a pipe
Being played by water, you shake it again lightly

And diminuendo runs through all its scales
Like a gutter stopping trickling. And now here comes
A sprinkle of drops out of the freshened leaves,

Then subtle little wets off grass and daisies;
Then glitter-drizzle, almost-breaths of air.
Up-end the stick again. What happens next

Is undiminished for having happened once,
Twice, ten, a thousand times before.
Who cares if all the music that transpires

Is the fall of grit or dry seeds through a cactus?
You are like a rich man entering heaven
Through the ear of a raindrop. Listen now again.

for Beth and Rand

Bagpipe Music

LOUIS MACNEICE

READ BY BOB GELDOF

It's no go the merrygoround, it's no go the rickshaw,
All we want is a limousine and a ticket for the peepshow.
Their knickers are made of crêpe-de-chine, their shoes are
made of python,
Their halls are lined with tiger rugs and their walls with heads
of bison.

John MacDonald found a corpse, put it under the sofa,
Waited till it came to life, and hit it with a poker,
Sold its eyes for souvenirs, sold its blood for whisky,
Kept its bones for dumb-bells to use when he was fifty.

It's no go the Yogi-Man, it's no go Blavatsky,
All we want is a bank balance and a bit of skirt in a taxi.

Annie MacDougall went to milk, caught her foot in the heather,
Woke to hear a dance record playing of Old Vienna.
It's no go your maidenheads, it's no go your culture,
All we want is a Dunlop tyre and the devil mend the puncture.

The Laird o' Phelps spent Hogmanay declaring he was sober,
Counted his feet to prove the fact and found he had one foot over.
Mrs Carmichael had her fifth, looked at the job with
repulsion,
Said to the midwife, 'Take it away; I'm through with over-production'.

It's no go the gossip column, it's no go the ceilidh,
All we want is a mother's help and a sugar-stick for the baby.

Bob Geldof is known in many guises: pop star, poet,
politician and media mogul. Bob Geldof was the
lead singer of the Boomtown Rats, but is best known
as the man behind Live Aid which raised over a
hundred million dollars worldwide for the famine in
Ethiopia. In 1986 Geldof received an honorary
knighthood for his charity efforts.

Willie Murray cut his thumb, couldn't count the damage,
Took the hide of an Ayrshire cow and used it for a bandage.
His brother caught three hundred cran when the seas were lavish,
Threw the bleeders back in the sea and went upon the parish.

It's no go the Herring Board, it's no go the Bible,
All we want is a packet of fags when our hands are idle.

It's no go the picture palace, it's no go the stadium,
It's no go the country cot with a pot of pink geraniums,
It's no go the Government grants, it's no go the elections,
Sit on your arse for fifty years and hang your hat on a pension.

It's no go my honey love, it's no go my poppet,
Work your hands from day to day, the winds will blow the profit.
The glass is falling hour by hour, the glass will fall for ever,
But if you break the bloody glass you won't hold up the weather.

Speaking to My father

THEO DORGAN

How should I now call up that man my father,
Who year after weary year went off to work,
Buried his heart beneath a weight of duty,
Buried himself early so that we might live?

How should I sit here and explain to his shade
That, yes, this is the work I do you died for,
This is the use I make of all that sacrifice,
I move the words as you moved heavy tyres.

True, there is no sickening stench of rubber,
No heat from the curing pans, no rage
At management, choked back by need as much as pride –
But father, the range of uselessness is wide.

Often, as I grew slowly, you'd let slip
A word, a helpless gesture or a look
That shook me to the roots, I'd sense the void
You stubbornly, heroically sweated back.

Now I have everything you lacked, above all
Freedom to shape the workload for the day –
It sounds like freedom, doesn't it? The truth is,
I hate the shiftwork just as much as you did.

There are days lately, as I thicken in years,
When I feel your sinews shift inside my frame,
I catch a look of yours in the mirror, shaving:
Mild, ironical, weary, a bit resigned –

Des Geraghty retired as General President of SIPTU, Ireland's largest trade union, in 2003 after a lifetime working in the trade union movement. Des is also an author and his works include *Luke Kelly*, a bestselling biography of the singer and socialist. He is a board member of Poetry Ireland.

But something else, too: your athlete's way
Of planting the feet carefully when troubled,
Shoulder square to the blow that may come,
Hands tense to defend what you hold dear.

What troubled you most? The question shies away
When I stab with my pen, clumsy as ever
– I don't even rightly know what troubles me,
Ignorant as when I rode upon your knee.

What would you make of me, I wonder, sitting here
Long after midnight, searching for the words to
Bring you back, soliciting the comfort of your shade
For the odd, useless creature that you made?

Here is the end of all that education,
The void is as close to me as it ever was to you,
I make poems of love as you and Rose made children,
Blindly, in hope and trust because I must.

Father, comrade, the same anger with the world
But not your patience moves me; I make you this,
A toy in words to re-introduce myself
And to ask, what must I do to be your child again?

Emotions

RORY GLEESON

READ BY BRENDAN GLEESON

I am a volcano, ready to erupt,
I am a three year old child at a Shakespeare play,
I am a caged bird, kept away from the world,
I am a squirrel in a field of nuts,
I am a child, at his first day at school,
I am a dog, trying to learn algebra,
I am all these emotions bundled in one, but most importantly
I am a person trying to finish this poem
Before the teacher kills me.

A former teacher, Brendan Gleeson spent the 1990s
earning an increasing amount of acclaim for his acting,
most notably in *The General* in 1998. Gleeson first
made an impression as an actor on audiences in the
role of Hamish, William Wallace's hulking ally in
Braveheart, in 1995. He lives in Dublin and his chosen
poem is by his son, Rory.

She Moved Through the Fair

PADRAIC COLUM

READ BY LARRY GOGAN

My young love said to me, 'My brothers won't mind,
And my parents won't slight you for your lack of kind.'
Then she stepped away from me, and this she did say,
'It will not be long, love, till our wedding day.'

She stepped away from me and she moved through the fair,
And fondly I watched her go here and go there,
Then she went her way homeward with one star awake,
As the swan in the evening moves over the lake.

The people were saying no two were e'er wed
But one had a sorrow that never was said,
And I smiled as she passed with her goods and her gear,
And that was the last that I saw of my dear.

I dreamt it last night that my young love came in,
So softly she entered, her feet made no din;
She came close beside me, and this she did say,
'It will not be long, love, till our wedding day.'

Larry Gogan is a presenter/producer with 2FM. He has
been voted No1 Music Presenter for 25 successive
years and his show has been the most listened to
music show on Irish radio and won many awards.

Seals at High Island

RICHARD MURPHY

The calamity of seals begins with jaws.
Born in caverns that reverberate
With endless malice of the sea's tongue
Clacking on shingle, they learn to bark back
In fear and sadness and celebration.
The ocean's mouth opens forty feet wide
And closes on a morsel of their rock.

Swayed by the thrust and backfall of the tide,
A dappled grey bull and a brindled cow
Copulate in the green water of a cove.
I watch from a cliff-top, trying not to move.
Sometimes they sink and merge into black shoals;
Then rise for air, his muzzle on her neck,
Their winged feet intertwined as a fishtail.

She opens her fierce mouth like a scarlet flower
Full of white seeds; she holds it open long
At the sunburst in the music of their loving;
And cries a little. But I must remember
How far their feelings are from mine marooned.
If there are tears at this holy ceremony
Theirs are caused by brine and mine by breeze.

Adrian Hardiman is one of Ireland's top legal minds. He
was born in Dublin and educated at University College
Dublin and the Kings Inns. He was called to the Bar in
1974, the Inner Bar in 1989 and appointed to the
Supreme Court in February 2000, one of the youngest
appointments ever to be made.

When the great bull withdraws his rod, it glows
Like a carnelian candle set in jade.
The cow ripples ashore to feed her calf;
While an old rival, eyeing the deed with hate,
Swims to attack the tired triumphant god.
They rear their heads above the boiling surf,
Their terrible jaws open, jetting blood.

At nightfall they haul out, and mourn the drowned,
Playing to the sea sadly their last quartet,
An improvised requiem that ravishes
Reason, while ripping scale up like a net;
Brings pity trembling down the rocky spine
Of headlands, till the bitter ocean's tongue
Swells in their cove, and smothers their sweet song.

Mary Harney was born in 1953 in Ballinasloe, Co Galway. She is leader of the Progressive Democrats, the political party she co-founded with Des O'Malley in 1985, and is also Tanaiste. A Trinity College graduate, she was the first woman in Ireland to lead a party into a coalition government.

Sunday's Well

VONA GROARKE

I
If, at night, I have the skylight open
it is only to admit a river
in which the silence of a city will converge
as chaos in the corners of my room.
This river, I say, will madden me.
This river will surely make me mad.

What will happen when morning has come
and my books and letters are washed up in the park?
Who will find my clothes and take them home?
How will I ever know my life again?

II
I've been dreaming again of an unlit room
where everything is clean and orderly:
a bed in the corner, a row of books,
a lover's photograph, clothes on a chair.
It needs only a woman to enter and say,
'I know this room. This room is mine.'

But no one comes. The silence holds.
Perhaps her body will be washed up in the park.
When morning comes, she will be found,
unknown and unidentified.

Christy Brown Came to Town

RICHARD HARRIS

READ BY RICHARD HARRIS

Christy Brown came to town riding on a wheelchair

Christy Brown came to town riding on a wheelchair
Back strapped to wheel and chair
Freewheeling down all his days
Into the byways in our heads
Visions bursting from his pen
Ink in blood, left foot in rapture
Riding through Fleet Street pulp
Past paper stand and paste
Ploughing stairs to heaven
Riding on and on and on
His chariot wheels
Conquering heroes in space
In the time allotted for his spin.
Reared in masses his childhood
Playpen on concrete slabs
Turned into flowing fountains
In his fountain pen toes
Ceasing to suffer in the kennel of his bark
Spent dark years with his ears
Tied to his mother's tongue.
Where are you mother?
I am here, I am here Christy
Growing flowers in your yard
Sending fruit to the marketplace in your soul
Patiently bending my breasts
To feed the hunger in your mind.
Dear bended lady
Drawing she drew in midnight whispers
The elements of verse
Vocalising grammar, building his armory for battle

Richard Harris was born in Limerick in 1930. He became a Hollywood superstar and his many memorable performances range from *The Sporting Life* in 1963 to *Gladiator* in 2000. As famous for his off-screen antics as his acting, Harris also loved literature and poetry. He died in October 2002.

Filling his long, sleepless, limping nights
With the music of her challenge
And she took a dead season from her womb
And built a birth as bright as Christmas.
In his schoolroom slum
That buried some and crippled most
The toast from her womb grew legs in her words
And walked long distance to the corners of the earth
Striding beyond Getsemane past the Avenue of the Sorrows
Out of Golgatha into resurrection.

Christy Brown came to town riding on a donkey

Christy Brown came to town riding on a donkey
Streets in palms carpeting his Sunday visit
He rode barebacked the donkey of the Apocalypse
Over bridges where crippled water stood still
In the lame shores of our crime.
He rode heaven high over tears and pity
Through the attending city
Where skeletons hid high in the cupboards of our complacency
He rode on and on and on and on he rode
On the laughter in his size
Everlasting in song
Storming our ears in wonder
Making his face shine upon us
And throwing from the seaweeds of his wisdom
Iodine
To heal the wounds of a waiting world.

How To Be My Heart

PAT BORAN

Become elastic,
enjoy the solo sound
as well as harmony.
Enjoy the fall –
don't expect ground.

Never move
but never quite be still.
See life as giving
rather than receiving
though the same blood passes
through your grasp like
rosaries, geometries, bound
infinities of love.

Be practical – work.
Keep the orchestra on course,
but imagine the clouds, the skies
you'll never see.

Learn trust. Don't mutiny
when I wade up to my chest in
   water.
Don't panic if I succumb to drugs
or drink. Don't sink.
Don't ache at every recollection
of a past populated by grief.
Don't succumb to disbelief.
Don't see only darkness up ahead.

Don't stay in bed all day.
Don't lie down and die.
Be there when I need the heart
to tell the unpalatable truth
or the necessary lie.

And give me the sensation of sky-
   diving
when she so much as
walks into my sight.
Make haemoglobin
while the sun shines.
But keep a little oxygen aside.

Starting out in RTE as a cameraman in the 1960's,
Shay Healy followed his interests in songwriting,
including penning the winning entry to Eurovision 1980 –
'What's Another Year' sung by Johnny Logan. Shay turned
his talents to the other side of the camera presenting many
programmes including the seminal off beat chat show
Nighthawks. Shay continues to make award-winning
documentaries which have included profiles on
comedian Dermot Morgan and musician Phil Lynott.

What Then?

W B YEATS

His chosen comrades thought at school
He must grow a famous man;
He thought the same and lived by rule,
All his twenties crammed with toil;
'What then?' sang Plato's ghost. 'What then?'

Everything he wrote was read,
After certain years he won
Sufficient money for his need,
Friends that have been friends indeed;
'What then?' sang Plato's ghost. 'What then?'

All his happier dreams came true –
A small old house, wife, daughter, son,
Grounds where plum and cabbage grew,
Poets and Wits about him drew;
'What then?' sang Plato's ghost. 'What then?'

'The work is done,' grown old he thought,
'According to my boyish plan;
Let the fools rage, I swerved in naught,
Something to perfection brought';
But louder sang that ghost, 'What then?'

READ BY SEAMUS HEANEY

Seamus Heaney was born in 1939 in Co Derry and lives
in Dublin. *Death of a Naturalist*, his first volume of poetry,
was published in 1966 and since then he has become
one of the leading poets of his generation. He was
Professor of Poetry at Oxford University from 1989 to
1994 and in 1995 he was awarded the Nobel Prize.

Dark Rosaleen

OWEN ROE MACWARD

TRANSLATED BY JAMES CLARENCE MANGAN

READ BY MICHAEL D HIGGINS

Michael D Higgins is a politician and author. Born in Limerick in 1941, Michael began his career as a lecturer at University College Galway. He has been a member of Seanead Eireann and was elected to Dail Eireann in 1987 where he continues to serve. He has been published extensively, with two poetry collections to date.

O, my Dark Rosaleen,
Do not sigh, do not weep!
The priests are on the ocean green,
They march along the Deep.
There's wine…from the royal pope,
Upon the ocean green;
And Spanish ale shall give you hope,
My Dark Rosaleen!
My own Rosaleen!
Shall glad your heart, shall give you
    hope,
Shall give you health, and help, and
    hope,
My Dark Rosaleen!

Over hills, and through dales,
Have I roamed for your sake;
All yesterday I sailed with sails
On river and on lake.
The Erne…at its highest flood,
I dashed across unseen,
For there was lightning in my blood,
My Dark Rosaleen!
My own Rosaleen!
Oh! There was lightning in my
    blood,
Red lightning lightened through my
    blood.
My Dark Rosaleen!

All day long, in unrest,
To and fro, do I move.
The very soul within my breast
Is wasted for you, love!
The heart…in my bosom faints
To think of you, my Queen,
My life of life, my saint of saints,
My Dark Rosaleen!
My own Rosaleen!
To hear your sweet and sad
    complaints,
My life, my love, my saint of saints,
My Dark Rosaleen!

Woe and pain, pain and woe,
Are my lot, night and noon,
To see your bright face clouded so,
Like to the mournful moon.
But yet…will I rear your throne
Again in golden sheen;
'Tis you shall reign, shall reign
    alone,
My Dark Rosaleen!
My own Rosaleen!
'Tis you shall have the golden
    throne,
'Tis you shall reign, and reign alone,
My Dark Rosaleen!

Over dews, over sands,
Will I fly, for your weal:
Your holy delicate white hands
Shall girdle me with steel
At home…in your emerald bowers,
From morning's dawn till e'en,
You'll pray for me, my flower of
    flowers,
My Dark Rosaleen!
My fond Rosaleen!
You'll think of me through
    Daylight's hours,
My virgin flower, my flower of
    flowers,
My Dark Rosaleen!

I could scale the blue air,
I could plough the high hills,
Oh, I could kneel all night in prayer,
To heal your many ills!
And one…beamy smile from you
Would float like light between
My toils and me, my own, my true,
My Dark Rosaleen!
My fond Rosaleen!
Would give me life and soul anew,
A second life, a soul anew,
My Dark Rosaleen!

O! the Erne shall run red
With redundance of blood,
The earth shall rock beneath our
    tread,
And flames wrap hill and wood,
And gun-peal, and slogan cry,
Wake many a glen serene.
Ere you shall fade, ere you shall die,
My Dark Rosaleen!
My own Rosaleen!
The Judgment Hour must first be
    nigh,
Ere you can fade, ere you can die,
My Dark Rosaleen!

Claudy

JAMES SIMMONS

READ BY JOHN HUME

John Hume was born in Derry in 1937. He was elected to the Stormont Parliament as an Independent in 1969. He went on to become a founder member of the SDLP party, serving as Deputy Leader and then Leader. Among his most notable achievements were his contributions in bringing about the IRA ceasefire and he was awarded the Nobel Prize for Peace in 1998 along with David Trimble.

The Sperrins surround it, the Faughan flows by,
at each end of Main Street the hills and the sky,
the small town of Claudy at ease in the sun
last July in the morning, a new day begun.

How peaceful and pretty if the moment could stop,
McIlhenny is straightening things in his shop,
and his wife is outside serving petrol, and then
a girl takes a cloth to a big window pane.

And McCloskey is taking the weight off his feet,
and McClelland and Miller are sweeping the street,
and, delivering milk at the Beaufort Hotel,
young Temple's enjoying his first job quite well.

And Mrs McLaughlin is scrubbing her floor,
and Artie Hone's crossing the street to a door,
and Mrs Brown, looking around for her cat,
goes off up an entry – what's strange about that?

Not much – but before she comes back to the road
that strange car parked outside her house will explode,
and all of the people I've mentioned outside
will be waiting to die or already have died.

An explosion too loud for your eardrums to bear,
and young children squealing like pigs in the square,
and all faces chalk-white and streaked with bright red,
and the glass and the dust and the terrible dead.

For an old lady's legs are ripped off, and the head
of a man's hanging open, and still he's not dead.
He is screaming for mercy, and his son stands and stares
and stares, and then suddenly, quick, disappears.

And Christ, little Katherine Aiken is dead,
and Mrs McLaughlin is pierced through the head.
Meanwhile to Dungiven the killers have gone,
and they're finding it hard to get through on the phone.

for Harry Barton, a song

I Grabbed an Education

PATRICK KAVANAGH

I wish I could be solemn as John Wayne
Making the matter-of-fact pay up and look fairly
Adequate copy for a new book, thoughtfully plain
So many words well put together squarely.
I wish I'd grabbed an education early.

Similarly when over Ted Hughes' work I pore
I am astonished at his animal knowledge
That Billy Smart would pay good money for;
He'd be an asset to a veterinary college.
Has Howard got a faculty in Dulwich?

One of these days I'm going to study hard
Save up a heap of words and spread them squarely
A shelf of poem books by the robot bard
And John will not review my works unfairly.
I grabbed an education late but barely.

READ BY NEIL JORDAN

Neil Jordan is Ireland's best known film director. He has directed such films as *The Company of Wolves*, *Mona Lisa*, *Interview with the Vampire*, *Michael Collins* and *The End of the Affair*. In 1992, *The Crying Game* was nominated for six Academy Awards, including Best Picture, and won Neil the Oscar for Best Original Screenplay.

All of These People

MICHAEL LONGLEY

READ BY FERGAL KEANE

Who was it who suggested that the opposite of war
Is not so much peace as civilisation? He knew
Our assassinated Catholic greengrocer who died
At Christmas in the arms of our Methodist minister,
And our ice-cream man whose continuing requiem
Is the twenty-one flavours children have by heart.
Our cobbler mends shoes for everybody; our butcher
Blends into his best sausages leeks, garlic, honey;
Our cornershop sells everything from bread to kindling.
Who can bring peace to people who are not civilised?
All of these people, alive or dead, are civilised.

Fergal Keane is the son of actor Eamon Keane and
nephew of the playwright John B Keane. He has been
a Special Correspondent for BBC News for ten years
and has reported from some of the world's major trouble
spots winning many awards. In 1996 Fergal was
awarded an OBE.

Stony Grey Soil

PATRICK KAVANAGH

READ BY FRANK KELLY

Frank Kelly played Father Jack Hackett in the TV series
Father Ted. Frank's film appearances range from *Ryan's
Daughter* to *Evelyn*. He has also written widely for TV
and radio. His hit single, *Christmas Countdown*,
charted three times in Britain and also reached No 1
in the Australian charts.

O stony grey soil of Monaghan
The laugh from my love you thieved;
You took the gay child of my passion
And gave me your clod-conceived.

You clogged the feet of my boyhood
And I believed that my stumble
Had the poise and stride of Apollo
And his voice my thick-tongued mumble.

You told me the plough was immortal!
O green-life-conquering plough!
Your mandril strained, your coulter blunted
In the smooth lea-field of my brow.

You sang on steaming dunghills
A song of coward's brood,
You perfumed my clothes with weasel itch,
You fed me on swinish food.

You flung a ditch on my vision
Of beauty, love and truth.
O stony grey soil of Monaghan
You burgled my bank of youth!

Lost the long hours of pleasure
All the women that love young men.
O can I still stroke the monster's back
Or write with unpoisoned pen

His name in these lonely verses
Or mention the dark fields where
The first gay flight of my lyric
Got caught in a peasant's prayer.

Mullahinsha, Drummeril, Black Shanco –
Wherever I turn I see
In the stony grey soil of Monaghan
Dead loves that were born for me.

Ulster Names

JOHN HEWITT

I take my stand by the Ulster names,
each clean hard name like a weathered stone;
Tyrella, Rostrevor, are flickering flames:
the names I mean are the Moy, Malone,
Strabane, Slieve Gullion and Portglenone.

Even suppose that each name were freed
from legend's ivy and history's moss,
there'd be music still, in say, Carrick-a-rede,
though men forget it's the rock across
the track of the salmon from Islay and Ross.

The names of a land show the heart of the race;
they move on the tongue like the lilt of a song.
You say the name and I see the place –
Drumbo, Dungannon, or Annalong.
Barony, townland, we cannot go wrong.

You say Armagh, and I see the hill
with the two tall spires or the square low tower;
the faith of Patrick is with us still;
his blessing falls in a moonlit hour,
when the apple orchards are all in flower.

You whisper Derry. Beyond the walls
and the crashing boom and the coiling smoke,
I follow that freedom which beckons and calls
to Colmcille tall in his grove of oak,
raising his voice for the rhyming folk.

County by county you number them over;
Tyrone, Fermanagh…I stand by a lake,
and the babbling curlew, the whistling plover
call over the whins in the chill daybreak
as the hills and the waters the first light take.

Let Down be famous for care-tilled earth,
for the little green hills and the harsh grey peaks,
the rocky bed of the Lagan's birth,
the white farm fat in the August weeks.
There's one more county my pride still seeks.

You give it the name and my quick thoughts run
through the narrow towns with their wheels of trade,
to Glenballyemon, Glenaan, Glendun,
from Trostan down to the braes of Layde
for there is the place where the pact was made.

But you have as good a right as I
To praise the place where your face is known,
for over us all is the selfsame sky;
the limestone's locked in the strength of the bone
and who shall mock at the steadfast stone?

So it's Ballinamallard, it's Crossmaglen,
It's Aughnacloy, it's Donaghadee,
It's Magherafelt breeds the best of men
I'll not deny it. But look for me
on the moss between Orra and Slievenanee.

The Singer's House

SEAMUS HEANEY

READ BY JOHN KELLY

When they said *Carrickfergus* I could hear
the frosty echo of saltminers' picks.
I imagined it, chambered and glinting,
A township built of light.

What do we say any more
to conjure the salt of our earth?
So much comes and is gone
that should be crystal and kept,

and amicable weathers
that bring up the grain of things,
their tang of season and store,
are all the packing we'll get.

So I say to myself *Gweebarra*
and its music hits off the place
like water hitting off granite.
I see the glittering sound

framed in your window,
knives and forks set on oilcloth,
and the seals' heads, suddenly outlined,
scanning everything.

People here used to believe
that drowned souls lived in the seals.
At spring tides they might change shape.
They loved music and swam in for a singer

who might stand at the end of summer
in the mouth of a whitewashed turf-shed,
his shoulder to the jamb, his song
a rowboat far out in evening.

When I came here first you were always singing,
a hint of the clip of the pick
in your winnowing climb and attack.
Raise it again, man. We still believe what we hear.

John Kelly is a writer and broadcaster. His novels include *The Little Hammer* and *Sophisticated Boom Boom*. He presents the award-winning show *Mystery Train* on RTE 1, and also the television arts review programme *The View*.

The Tree Speaks

CATHAL Ó SEARCAIGH

TRANSLATED BY ANNA NÍ DHOMHNAILL

READ BY BRIAN KENNEDY

I am the tree that will be destroyed,
tomorrow I will be cut and laid low.

My dignity will be hacked at;
my limbs will be strewn
in the dirt of the street —
my strong limbs.
The white blossom of my laugh will be stolen.

Everything I have stored
in the marrow of memories will be destroyed;
my first tears of joy; my first leaves of hope;
the first syllable of music pulsing through my branches;
the first Spring which clothed me in a green dress.

The tales of adventure related to me
by the birds; the nests that flourished
in the leafy shelter of my eye,
the storms I calmed
in the softness of my embrace.

The children who swung between life and eternity
in my branches; the whispered secrets
breathed to me in the night shadows;
the moon who dressed me in the golden lace of autumn;
the angels who alighted on me with the snow.

Brian Kennedy is one of Ireland's most successful
ambassadors of music. His number one award-winning
album 'A Better Man' put three of his albums in the
Irish Top 30 simultaneously. His BBC TV series *Brian
Kennedy on Song* traces the roots of Irish songs. The
accompanying CD – his seventh – has already
gone gold.

With the fluent tongue of my leaves
I defended, passionately,
this space in which I thrive;
in which I spread with wonder
the green thoughts that come to me in Spring.

With bounteous seeds I covered
this earthly space around me with certainty,
in celebration of the Tree Spirit
that quickened firmly in me
as I came of age.

And tomorrow when they burn me,
when my bones will smoke,
I will become one with the Sky, the Fiery Sky!
that has fuelled my imagination from dawn to dusk
with brightness, with Light.

The Fiddler of Dooney

W B YEATS

When I play on my fiddle in Dooney,
Folk dance like a wave of the sea;
My cousin is a priest in Kilvarnet,
My brother in Moharabuiee.

I passed my brother and cousin:
They read in their books of prayer;
I read in my book of songs
I bought at the Sligo fair.

When we come at the end of time,
To Peter sitting in state,
He will smile on the three old spirits,
But call me first through the gate;

For the good are always the merry,
Save by an evil chance,
And the merry love the fiddle,
And the merry love to dance:

And when the folk there spy me,
They will all come up to me,
With 'Here is the fiddler of Dooney!'
And dance like a wave of the sea.

To A Child

PATRICK KAVANAGH

Child do not go
Into the dark places of the soul,
For there the grey wolves whine,
The lean grey wolves.

I have been down
Among the unholy ones who tear
Beauty's white robe and clothe her
In rags of prayer.

Child there is light somewhere
Under a star,
Sometime it will be for you
A window that looks
Inward to God.

Sister Stanislaus Kennedy is an Irish Sister of Charity and
a member of the Irish Council of State. Campaigner,
innovator, publisher and lecturer, she is the founder of
Focus Ireland, one of the leading agencies combating
homelessness in Ireland.

My Father

JOHN B KEANE

READ BY BRENDAN KENNELLY

Brendan Kennelly has published poetry, plays, novels and
critical essays. He is Professor of Modern Literature at
Trinity College Dublin. He has published more than
20 volumes of poems and has won the AE Memorial
Prize for Poetry and the Critics Special Harvey Award.

When he spoke gustily and sincerely
Spittle fastened
Not merely upon close lapel
But nearly blinded
Those who had not hastened
To remove pell-mell.
He was inviolate.
Clung to old stoic principle,
And he
Dismissed his weaknesses
As folly.
His sinning was inchoate;
Drank ill-advisedly.
His waistcoat I remember –
Tobacco-perfumed parallelogram
Of pennied pockets.
Once, when unexpected telegram
Advised immediate payment
Eyes rocketed in sockets
At demand of claimant.
He wired this cant:
"Coffers, rent apart.
Am intimate friend
Of Weller, Tony.
Have ripped beadles apart.
Am, sir, compelled to dial
The number of your heart."
I am terribly proud of my father,
Bitterly, faithfully proud.
Let none say a word to my father
Or mention his name out loud.
I adored his munificent blather
Since I was his catch-as-catch-can.
I am terribly proud of my father
For he was a loveable man.

Antarctica

DEREK MAHON

'I am just going outside and may be some time.'
The others nod, pretending not to know.
At the heart of the ridiculous, the sublime.

He leaves them reading and begins to climb,
Goading his ghost into the howling snow;
He is just going outside and may be some time.

The tent recedes beneath its crust of rime
And frostbite is replaced by vertigo:
At the heart of the ridiculous, the sublime.

Need we consider it some sort of crime,
This numb self-sacrifice of the weakest? No,
He is just going outside and may be some time –

In fact, for ever. Solitary enzyme,
Though the night yield no glimmer there will glow,
At the heart of the ridiculous, the sublime.

He takes leave of the earthly pantomime
Quietly, knowing it is time to go.
'I am just going outside and may be some time.'
At the heart of the ridiculous, the sublime.

for Richard Ryan

Pat Kenny presents the morning radio programme *Today
with Pat Kenny* and hosts the Friday night television show
The Late Late Show. He has also worked as a presenter
of mainstream current affairs programmes.

Thems Your Mammy's Pills

LELAND BARDWELL

They'd scraped the top soil off the garden
and every step or two they'd hurled a concrete block
bolsters of mud like hippos from the hills
rolled on the planters plantings of the riff-raff of the city.

The schizophrenic planners had finished off their job
folded their papers, put away their pens –
the city clearances were well ahead.

And all day long a single child was crying
while his father shouted: Don't touch them,
Thems your mammy's pills.

I set to work with zeal to play 'Doll's House',
'Doll's life', 'Doll's Garden'
while my adolescent sons played Temporary Heat
in the living room out front
and drowned the opera of admonitions:
Don't touch them, thems your mammy's pills.

Fragile as needles the women wander forth
laddered with kids, the unborn one ahead
to forge the mile through mud and rut
where mulish earth-removers rest, a crazy sculpture.

They are going back to the city for the day
this is all they live for –
going back to the city for the day.

The line of shops and solitary pub
are camouflaged like check points on the border
the supermarket stretches emptily
a circus of sausages and time
the till-girl gossips in the veg department

Once in a while a woman might come in
to put another pound on
the electronic toy for Christmas.

From behind the curtains every night
the video lights are flickering, butcher blue
Don't touch them, thems your mammy's pills.

No one has a job in Killinarden
nowadays they say it is a no go area
I wonder, then, who goes and does not go
in this strange forgotten world
of video and valium

I visited my one time neighbour
not so long ago. She was sitting
in the hangover position
I knew she didn't want to see me
although she'd cried when we were leaving

I went my way
through the quietly rusting motor cars and prams
past the barricades of wire, the harmony of junk.
The babies that I knew are punk-size now
and soon children will have children
and new voices ring the *leit motif.*

Don't touch them, thems your mammy's pills.

for Edward McLachlan

Ómós do John Millington Synge

MÁIRTIN Ó DIREÁIN

An toisc a thug tú chun mo dhaoine
Ón gcein mheith don charraig gharbh
Ba cheile lei an chré bheo
Is an leid a scéith as léan is danaid.

Nior eistis scéal na gcloch,
Bhi eacht i scéal an teallaigh,
Nior speis leat leac na cill,
Ni thig éamh as an gcré mharbh.

Do dhuinigh Deirdre romhat sa ród
Is curach Naoise do chas Ceann Gainimh,
D'imigh Deirdre is Naoise leo
Is chaith Peigin le Seáinin aithis.

An leabhar ba ghnáth i do dhóid
As ar chuiris breithe ar marthain;
Ghabh Deirdre, Naoise is Peigin cló
Is thug léim ghaisce de na leathanaigh.

Tá cleacht mo dhaoine ag meath,
Ni cabhair feasta an tonn mar fhalla,
Ach go dtaga Coill Chuain go hInis Meáin
Beidh na bréithre a chnuasais trath
Ar marthain fós i dteanga eachtrann.

Mick Lally appeared on Irish TV screens every Sunday night for 22 years in the soap opera *Glenroe*. He was involved with the founding of Galway's world-renowned Druid theatre company in 1975 and has appeared in many of its productions.

Homage to John Millington Synge

MÁIRTIN Ó DIREÁIN

The impulse that brought you to my people
From the distant pasture to the harsh rock
Was partnered by the living clay
And the intimations of loss and sorrow.

You didn't listen to the tale of the stones,
Greatness lived in the tale of the hearth,
You paid no heed to tombstone or graveyard,
No whimper escapes the lifeless dust.

Deirdre appeared before you on the road
And Naoise's currach weathered Ceann Gainimh;
Deirdre and Naoise went to their death
And Pegeen flung abuse at Shawneen.

The book was always in your hand
You brought the words in it to life;
Deirdre, Naoise and Pegeen took form
And leaped like heroes from the pages.

The ways of my people decay,
The sea no longer serves as a wall,
But till Coill Chuain comes to Inis Meáin
The words you gathered then
Will live on in an alien tongue.

There are Days

JOHN MONTAGUE

There are days when
one should be able
to pluck off one's head
like a dented or worn
helmet, straight from
the nape and collarbone
(those crackling branches!)

and place it firmly down
in the bed of a flowing stream.
Clear, clean, chill currents
coursing and spuming through
the sour and stale compartments
of the brain, dimmed eardrums,
bleared eyesockets, filmed tongue.

And then set it back again
on the base of the shoulders:
well tamped down, of course,
the laved skin and mouth,
the marble of the eyes
rinsed and ready
for love; for prophecy?

for Lawrence Sullivan

Desmond Lynam, born in Ennis, Co Clare, was the BBC's
main sports anchorman for over 20 years, presenting
Match of the Day and all major sporting events including
the Olympics, Wimbledon, the World Cup and the
Grand National. In 1999, Des moved to ITV to present
its live football coverage.

The Sunlight on the Garden

LOUIS MACNEICE

The sunlight on the garden
Hardens and grows cold,
We cannot cage the minute
Within its nets of gold,
When all is told
We cannot beg for pardon.

Our freedom as free lances
Advances towards its end;
The earth compels, upon it
Sonnets and birds descend;
And soon, my friend,
We shall have no time for dances.

The sky was good for flying
Defying the church bells
And every evil iron
Siren and what it tells;
The earth compels,
We are dying, Egypt, dying

And not expecting pardon,
Hardened in heart anew,
But glad to have sat under
Thunder and rain with you,
And grateful too
For sunlight on the garden.

READ BY JOHN LYNCH

John Lynch first gained notice in 1984 with his
portrayal of a terrorist who falls for an older woman in
Pat O'Connor's film *Cal*. He played a leading role in
In the Name of the Father and has starred in such films
as *Sliding Doors*, *Some Mother's Son* and *Evelyn*.

To A May Baby

WINIFRED M LETTS

To come at tulip time how wise!
Perhaps you will not now regret
The shining gardens, jewel set,
Of your first home in Paradise
Nor fret
Because you may not quite forget.

To come at swallow-time how wise!
When every bird has built a nest;
Now you may fold your wings and rest
And watch this new world with surprise;
A guest
For whom the earth has donned her best.

To come when life is gay how wise!
With lambs and every happy thing
That frisks on foot or sports on wing,
With daisies and with butterflies,
But Spring
Had nought so sweet as you to bring.

Ciaran MacMathuna joined RTE in 1954 with special
responsibility for Irish traditional music and song on radio.
He is best known for RTE's most enduring radio show *Mo
Cheol Thu*, the Sunday morning bilingual programme of
music, song and poetry which has been running for over
30 years.

I Will Go With My Father

JOSEPH CAMPBELL

READ BY JIMMY MAGEE

I will go with my father a-ploughing
To the green field by the sea,
And the rooks and the crows and the seagulls
Will come flocking after me.
I will sing to the patient horses
With the lark in the white of the air,
And my father will sing the plough-song
That blesses the cleaving share.

I will go with my father a-sowing
To the red field by the sea,
And the rooks and the gulls and the starlings
Will come flocking after me.
I will sing to the striding sowers
With the finch on the flowering sloe,
And my father will sing the seed-song
That only the wise men know.

I will go with my father a-reaping
To the brown field by the sea,
And the geese and the crows and the children
Will come flocking after me.
I will sing to the weary reapers
With the wren in the heat of the sun,
And my father will sing the scythe-song
That joys for the harvest done.

Jimmy Magee began his broadcasting career on Radio
Eireann's *Junior Sports Magazine* and has commentated
on every Olympic Games since Munich in 1972 as well
as FA Cups, soccer internationals and World Cups.
Jimmy is the regular presenter of Radio 1's *Sunday Sport*
and also writes a column for the *Sunday World*.

Requiem for the Croppies

SEAMUS HEANEY

READ BY TOMMY MAKEM

The pockets of our greatcoats full of barley –
No kitchens on the run, no striking camp –
We moved quick and sudden in our own country.
The priest lay behind ditches with the tramp.
A people, hardly marching – on the hike –
We found new tactics happening each day:
We'd cut through reins and rider with the pike
And stampede cattle into infantry,
Then retreat through hedges where cavalry must be thrown.
Until, on Vinegar Hill, the fatal conclave.
Terraced thousands died, shaking scythes at cannon.
The hillside blushed, soaked in our broken wave.
They buried us without shroud or coffin
And in August the barley grew up out of the grave.

Tommy Makem has written hundreds of songs, many of which have become standards in the repertoire of folk singers around the world. During the 13 years Tommy performed with The Clancy Brothers, they brought Irish music to the attention of audiences worldwide.

The Country Fiddler

JOHN MONTAGUE

READ BY PADDY MOLONEY

My uncle played the fiddle – more elegantly the violin –
A favourite at barn and crossroads dance,
He knew 'The Morning Star' and 'O'Neill's Lament'.

Bachelor head of a house full of sisters,
Runner of poor racehorses, spendthrift,
He left for the New World in an old disgrace.

He left his fiddle in the rafters
When he sailed, never played afterwards,
A rural art stilled in the discord of Brooklyn.

A heavily-built man, tranquil-eyed as an ox,
He ran a wild speakeasy, and died of it.
During the Depression many dossed in his cellar.

I attended his funeral in the Church of the Redemption,
Then, unexpected successor, reversed time
To return where he had been born.

During my schooldays the fiddle rusted
(The bridge fell away, the catgut snapped)
Reduced to a plaything, stinking of stale rosin.

The country people asked if I also had music
(All the family had had) but the fiddle was in pieces
And the rafters remade, before I discovered my craft.

Twenty years afterwards, I saw the church again,
And promised to remember my burly godfather
And his rural craft after this fashion:

So succession passes, through strangest hands.

Paddy Moloney is the founder and leader of The Chieftains. In the forty years since he founded the group, they have played across the world, and won a panoply of awards, including six Grammys, an Emmy and an Oscar.

Christ Goodbye

PADRAIC FIACC

READ BY EAMON McCANN

Dandering home from work at midnight
They tripped him up on a ramp
Asked him if he were a Catholic
A wee bit soft in the head he was
The last person in the world
You'd want to hurt
His arms and legs broken
His genitals roasted
With a shipyard worker's blowlamp.

In all the stories that the Christian Brothers
Tell you of Christ.
He never screamed like this.
Surely this is not the way to
Show a manly bearing
Screaming for them to please stop
And then later like screaming for death.

When they made him wash the stab wounds at the sink
They kept on hammering him with the pickaxe handle
Then they pulled Christ's trousers down
Threatening to cut off his balls.
Poor boy Christ.
For when they finally got round to finishing him off
By shooting him in the back of the head
The poor Fenian fucker
Was already dead.

Eamon McCann was born in 1943. He is a civil rights
activist, a journalist, broadcaster and trade unionist.

Literary History

RITA KELLY

Strange that Miller from Mountrath
should have let Heaney slip
out of the domain of his Dolmen.
Backed a different horse
went with a man much more morose,
you could never imagine him saying
he loved being a Disc Jockey, for Chrissake,
at the solemn end of the spectrum.

I remember Miller too,
the bearded one, the barbarian,
hoi barbari, the clipped prickly kind of beard,
standing on the narrow passage
that is Middle Street, in Galway,
sometime in the 1970s,
having come out of the golden-peacocked curtained
MacLiammoired Taibhdhearc.

Who now knows what play it was which delved
into the depths of perceived dullness.
Who cares, who remembers,
just the outstretched arms of Miller
and the voice taking in all
the boom of a dry-boned and dead past:
Was it for this the wild geese
did whatever they did and fled
was it for this Lord Edward died?

Ah, looking back, always looking back
to Ballylee, to Ballyhoo, to anything back there,
uneasing us in our presentations and in our productions,
mad gone and long gone,
the miserable and the belligerent
O'Leary and the grave.

The great tradition.
Keeping everything intact, the confused thinking
and the half-thinking, wearing facial hair,
some kind of modish mannerism,
and that it was all *ipso facto* better then.

But the clean-shaven Athenian
comes running down the furrow,
yapping after his father,
running down from Co Derry,
farming stock, from the hot Gates of Thermopylae,
running against the destructive forces of time
and obliteration
with a narrative and an ethical form of memory,
with multifarious narrations and nuances.

But Miller from Mountrath,
under the spartan design
of his ancient passage grave
like the Lacedaemonian child
left out on the roof to harden off,
fails.

While our Athenian rides out like Arion
on the smooth back of the dolphin
to wash the further shores with song
having mesmerized the greedy sailors

The Game of Your life

GABRIEL FITZMAURICE

READ BY PAUL McGRATH

Whatever way it's kicked out, face the ball!
While wingers await delivery in space,
Centrefield must rise above the maul
And safely field, taking thought to place
The ball of fortune with the chosen one
And will him on to make the greatest use
Of what he's given as he solos on;
Centrefield's involved as play ensues.
For now's the time when great men must redeem
The story of the game from death, defeat:
The game of life's the story of a team
Who cannot rest until their task's complete
To take the cup, the cup that cannot pass
And raise it up in glory for the mass.

for Bernard O'Donohue

Paul McGrath is one of Ireland's most acclaimed
footballing heroes. He played for his country on 83
occasions, including perhaps Ireland's greatest victory,
beating Italy in World Cup 1994. A former Manchester
United player, he was voted Aston Villa's Player of the
Millennium in 2000.

Shapes and Shadows

DEREK MAHON

READ BY PAUL McGUINNESS

William Scott, oil on canvas, Ulster Museum

The kitchens would grow bright
in blue frames; outside, still
harbour and silent cottages,
from a time of shortages,
shapes deft and tranquil,
black kettle and black pot.

Too much the known structures
those simple manufactures,
communion of frying pans,
skinny beans and spoons,
colander and fish-slice
in a polished interior space.

But tension of hand and heart
abstracted the growing art
to a dissonant design
and a rich dream of paint,
on the grim basic plan
a varied white pigment

knifed and scrubbed, in one
corner a boiling brown
study in mahogany;
beige-biscuit left; right
a fat patch of white,
bread and milk in agony.

Rough brushwork here, thick
but vague; for already
behind these there loom
shades of the prehistoric,
ghosts of colour and form,
furniture, function, body –

as if to announce the death
of preconception and myth
and start again on the fresh
first morning of the world
with snow, ash, whitewash,
limestone, mother-of-pearl,

bleach, paper, soap and foam,
top-of-the milk cream,
to find in the nitty-gritty
of surfaces and utensils
the shadow of a presence
a long-sought community.

Paul McGuinness has been U2's manager since their
early days. He also manages P J Harvey and co-founded
record label Celtic Heartbeat, which counts *Riverdance*
as one of its most notable successes.

The People I Grew Up With Were Afraid

MICHAEL GORMAN

The people I grew up with were afraid.
They were alone too long in waiting-rooms,
in dispensaries and in offices whose functions
they did not understand.

To buck themselves up, they thought
of lost causes, of 'Nature-boy'
O'Dea who tried to fly
from his bedroom window;
of the hunch-backed, little typist
who went roller-skating at Strandhill.
Or, they re-lived the last afternoon
of Benny Kirwin, pale, bald,
Protestant shop-assistant in Lyons' drapery.
One Wednesday, the town's half-day,
he hanged himself from a tree
on the shore at Lough Gill.

And what were they afraid of? Rent
collectors, rate collectors, insurance men.
Things to do with money. But,
especially of their vengeful God.
On her death-bed, Ena Phelan prayed
that her son would cut his hair.

Sometimes, they return to me,
Summer lunchtimes, colcannon
for the boys, back-doors
of all the houses open, the
news blaring on the radios.
Our mother's factory pay-packet
is sitting in the kitchen press
and our father, without
humour or relief, is
waiting for the sky to fall.

Solstice

GERRY DAWE

You arrived that bad winter
when I was like a man
walking in a circle no one else was near.

The lakes behind had frozen,
from the dump gulls came and went
and the news was all discontent,

of *Sell-out* and blame for the dead
country-boy faces that already were
fading from church wall and gate,

but the seas tightened their grip
when you faced the light and let rip
a first cry of bewilderment

at this beginning, the snow
buttressed against brilliant windows,
and where they washed you clean

I saw the ice outside fall
and imagined the fires burning
on the Hill of Tara ring

across the concealed earth
towards a silent hospital
and our standing still

all around you, Olwen,
transfixed by your birth
in such a bitter season.

for my daughter

READ BY VAN MORRISON

Van Morrison's musical career spans more than four decades. He has produced over 20 studio albums and gained iconic status in Ireland and internationally with albums such as 'Astral Weeks' and 'Poetic Champions Compose'.

The Village Schoolmaster
from *The Deserted Village*

OLIVER GOLDSMITH

READ BY MIKE MURPHY

Beside yon straggling fence that skirts the way
With blossom'd furze unprofitably gay,
There, in his noisy mansion, skill'd to rule,
The village master taught his little school;
A man severe he was, and stern to view,
I knew him well, and every truant knew;
Well had the boding tremblers learn'd to trace
The days disasters in his morning face;
Full well they laugh'd with counterfeited glee,
At all his jokes, for many a joke had he:
Full well the busy whisper, circling round,
Convey'd the dismal tidings when he frown'd:
Yet he was kind; or if severe in aught,
The love he bore to learning was in fault.
The village all declar'd how much he knew;
'twas certain he could write, and cipher too:
Lands he could measure, terms and tides presage,
And e'en the story ran that he could gauge.
In arguing too, the parson own'd his skill,
For e'en though vanquish'd he could argue still;
While words of learned length and thund'ring sound
Amazed the gazing rustics rang'd around;
And still they gaz'd and still the wonder grew,
That one small head could carry all he knew.

Mike Murphy has hosted a string of successful TV and radio shows which have earned him a number of broadcasting awards. He is best known as presenter of RTE's flagship radio programme *The Arts Show* which he hosted for 11 years.

Fontenoy

EMILY LAWLESS

I – Before the Battle; night

Oh bad the march, the weary march, beneath these alien skies,
But good the night, the friendly night, that soothes our tired eyes.
And bad the war, the tedious war, that keeps us sweltering here,
But good the hour, the friendly hour, that brings the battle near.
That brings us on the battle, that summons to their share
The homeless troops, the banished men, the exiled sons of Clare.

Oh little Corca Bascinn, the wild, the bleak, the fair!
Oh little stony pastures, whose flowers are sweet, if rare!
Oh rough and rude Atlantic, the thunderous, the wide,
Whose kiss is like a soldier's kiss which will not be denied!
The whole night long we dream of you, and waking think we're there, –
Vain dream, and foolish waking, we never shall see Clare.

The wind is wild to-night, there's battle in the air;
The wind is from the west, and it seems to blow from Clare.
Have you nothing, nothing for us, loud brawler of the night?
No news to warm our heart-strings, to speed us through the fight?
In this hollow, star-pricked darkness, as in the sun's hot glare,
In sun-tide, moon-tide, star-tide, we thirst, we starve for Clare!

Hark! yonder through the darkness one distant rat-tat-tat!
The old foe stirs out there, God bless his soul for that!
The old foe musters strongly, he's coming on at last,
And Clare's Brigade may claim its own wherever blows fall fast.
Send us, ye western breezes, our full, our rightful share,
For Faith, and Fame, and Honour, and the ruined hearths of Clare.

II – After the Battle; early dawn, Clare coast

'Mary mother, shield us! Say, what men are ye,
Sweeping past so swiftly on this morning sea?'
'Without sails or rowlocks merrily we glide
Home to Corca Bascinn on the brimming tide.'

Jesus save you, gentry! why are ye so white,
Sitting all so straight and still in this misty light?'
'Nothing ails us, brother; joyous souls are we
Sailing home together, on the morning sea.'

'Cousins, friends, and kinsfolk, children of the land,
Here we come together, a merry, rousing band;
Sailing home together from the last great fight,
Home to Clare from Fontenoy, in the morning light.

'Men of Corca Bascinn, men of Clare's Brigade,
Harken, stony hills of Clare, hear the charge we made;
See us come together, singing from the fight,
Home to Corca Bascinn, in the morning light.'

The View From Under the Table

PAULA MEEHAN

READ BY CHRISTINA NOBLE

The view from under the table
was the best view and the table itself kept the sky
from falling. The world was fringed with red velvet tassels;
whatever play ran in that room the tablecloth was curtains for.
I was the audience. Listen to me laughing. Listen
to me weeping. I was a child. What did I know?
Except that the moon was a porcelain globe and swung from a brass chain. O
that wasn't the moon at all. The moon was my true love. Oak was my roof and
under the table no one could see you. My granny could see me.
Out, she'd say. Out. And up on her lap the smell of kitchen and sleep.
She'd rock me. She'd lull me. No one was kinder.

What ails you child? I never told her. Not
one word would cross my lips. Shadows I'd say. I don't like the shadows.
They're waiting to snatch me. There at the turn of the stairs.
On the landing. To the right of the wardrobe. In the fridge, white ghosts.
Black ghosts in the coal shed. In the bread bin, hungry ghosts.

Somewhere, elsewhere, my mother was sulking in the rain. I call up
her young face. Who did she think she was with her big words
and her belt and her beatings? Who do I think I am to write her?
She must have been sad. She must have been lonely.
Discipline. Chastisement. I stretch out my four year old hands.

Christina Noble grew up in poverty in Dublin during the
1940s. In 1989, driven by the memory of her own
childhood, Christina travelled to Vietnam and began
working with the street children. In 1990, the Christina
Noble Children's Foundation was established and has
helped more than 184,000 children in Vietnam and
Mongolia.

A Kind of Trust

BRENDAN KENNELLY

I am happy now.
You rose from your sick bed
After three weeks. Your heart was
   low

When the world grew small,
A white ceiling
And four yellow walls.

Let me say again what this means
To me. As far as I know
Love always begins

Like a white morning
Of seagulls near the window,
Messengers bringing

Word that we must up and out
Into a small garden
Where there are late

Apples we shall find
So ripe that the slightest touch
Will pitch them to the ground.

Best things seem content to fall and
   fail.
I am not good enough for that.
I fight the drag and pull

Of any kind of dying
And bitterly insist
On that white morning

When you weakly climb the stairs,
Letting new life reach you like a gift
There at the brown bannister.

I do not insist
Out of panic or vague dread
But out of a kind of trust

In this beginning
With late apples and early seagulls
And a young sun shining

When you let cold water flow into a
   cup,
Steady yourself between two chairs
And stand straight up.

Michael Noonan has been active in politics since 1974
when he was elected to Limerick County Council. He was
leader of the Fine Gael Party from 2001 to 2002 and
has held the positions of Minister for Justice, for Industry
and Commerce, for Energy and for Health.

The Jackeen's Lament for the Blaskets

BRENDAN BEHAN

TRANSLATED BY DONAGH MACDONAGH

The sea will be under the sun like an empty mirror,
No boat under sail, no sign of a living sinner
And nothing reflected but one golden eagle, the last,
On the edge of the world beyond the lonely Blaskets.

The sun will be setting, the shadows of night dispersing
As the rising moon shines down through the sea-cold night cloud,
Her long, bare fingers stretched down to the empty earth
And the houses fallen and ruined and broken apart.

The only sounds the hush of the birds' soft feathers
Skimming over the water, returning safe and together,
And the wind as it sighs and softly swings the half-door
Mourning a hearth that is cold for ever more.

David Norris is a politician, academic, Joycean scholar,
performer and gay rights campaigner. As a Senator,
representing Trinity College, David is known for his work
on a range of controversial issues.

A Woman Untouched

FRANK MCGUINNESS

I

I am flying to California on Virgin Airlines
When the death of Helen is announced in Ireland.

Let the sky turn metallic and weep buckets.
Let my hands be raised in supplication.

It cannot be so. Most beautiful Helen.
I am not prepared for her eternity.

She the loveliest, the most gentle of women.
She the funniest, the best of all times.

Helen is dead. Let the heavens rip open
The veil of the temple of the sweet Atlantic.

Is that her soul ascending? Helen.
There is laughter in the whole happiness

Of your friendship. For your thirty-three years.
You have graced this earth. Grace the air I fly.

Give me strength through grace to say savage words.
Helen is dead. Helen of Troy is dead.

Miriam O'Callaghan presents RTE's flagship current affairs
programme *Prime Time*. She has chaired a number of
high-profile debates, including the last Presidential
debate. Before joining RTE, Miriam worked for ten years
in British television, seven of these as a reporter for
BBC2's *Newsnight*.

II

She moved through life like a woman untouched.
Her radiant face concealed its secrets.
When she chose to speak, there was wisdom stirring.
She kept her counsel, she believed in fate.

Believing in wisdom, she faced it squarely.
Poor fate didn't know what it had taken on.
All fights, my friend, are fights to the bitter end.
As soon stop the sun shining as the end be sweet.

III

You say I was beautiful – and I was.
Yet beauty is a mask of beaten gold.
I might approve of this appellation,
This Helen of Troy, were it ever true.
But it's not. So, call me by my own name.
Say it, even if it breaks your heart.
Do you not think my heart is broken?
Do you think mythology eases my pained heart?
One day I looked at myself in a mirror.
The loveliest woman in Ireland looked out at me.
I told her where to get off that instant.
I'm a working woman, I've a job to do.
That woman in the mirror then laughed like myself.
My strength is that I can see through myself.

IV

The spring is coming to California:
In Booterstown Avenue a palm tree grows.

Exotic growth, no place to be here,
Like yourself, Anne O'Callaghan.

No chance now it will ever be uprooted
From shading my house. Dance on its leaves and

Let your soul ascend as a tree ascends.
I phone Kaye Fanning from California.

She said, she's dead, our loved girl is dead.
I cried for an hour in a motel room.

Early morning there, late night at home.
I went out and taught Anton Chekhov. *Three Sisters.*

I call on the sister of the spring that comes
To California, of the palm tree that grows

In Booterstown Avenue, flying on Virgin Airlines,
The sky turned metallic and weeping buckets.

She the loveliest, the most gentle of women,
She the funniest, the best of all times,

Helen is dead. Let the heavens rip open
The veil of the temple of the sweet Atlantic.

Pride

PAUL WILLIAMS

They called him a 'Molly', his family
Every day
Every week
Every year.
And still they were shocked when he told them
Your son
Your brother
Is queer.
As if he had committed a murder
Or a crime that they just couldn't bear
When he walked into their local pub
They walked out
Leaving him there.

He stood in a room full of strangers
His new boyfriend by his side
Emotionally numbed for an instant
He reached in and regained his pride.
A new pride emerged
One that carries today
When they run away from reality
He is proud to be gay.

READ BY SINEAD O'CONNOR

Sinead O'Connor was catapulted to fame with the success of *Nothing Compares to U*, written by Prince. Since then Sinead's uncompromising stances on a variety of issues have placed her at the centre of media and public debate.

Poem From a Three Year Old

BRENDAN KENNELLY

READ BY DANIEL O'DONNELL

And will the flowers die?

And will the people die?

And every day do you grow old, do I
grow old, no I'm not old, do
flowers grow old?

Old things – do you throw them
out?

Do you throw old people out?

And how you know a flower that's
old?

The petals fall, the petals fall from
flowers,
and do the petals fall from people
too,
every day more petals fall until the
floor where I would like to play I
want to play is covered with old
flowers and people all the same
together lying there with petals
fallen
on the dirty floor I want to play
the floor you come and sweep
with the huge broom.

The dirt you sweep, what happens
that,
what happens all the dirt you sweep
from flowers and people, what
happens all the dirt? Is all the
dirt what's left of flowers and
people, all the dirt there in a
heap under the huge broom that
sweeps everything away?

Why you work so hard, why brush
and sweep to make a heap of dirt?
And who will bring new flowers?
And who will bring new people?
   Who will
bring new flowers to put in water
where no petals fall on to the
floor where I would like to
play? Who will bring new flowers
that will not hang their heads
like tired old people wanting sleep?
Who will bring new flowers that
do not split and shrivel every
day? And if we have new flowers,
will we have new people too to
keep the flowers alive and give
them water?

And will the new young flowers die?

And will the new young people die?

And why?

Daniel O'Donnell is one of Ireland's most popular exports.
Hailing from Donegal, he has surpassed sales of
five million albums and 1.5 million videos and his sell-out
concert appearances have taken him from New York's
Carnegie Hall to Sydney's Opera House.

Plaisir D'Amour

PATRICK GALVIN

Spring
My father
Against the victories of age
Would not concede defeat
He dyed his hair
And when my mother called
He said he wasn't there.

My mother, too
Fought back against the years
But in her Sunday prayers
Apologised to God.
My father said there was no God
'And that one knows it to her painted toes'.

My mother smiled.
She'd plucked her eyebrows too
And wore a see-through skirt
With matching vest.
'He likes French knickers best' she said
'I'll have them blest'.

My father raged.
He liked his women young, he said
And not half-dead.
He bought a second-hand guitar he couldn't play
And sang the only song he knew –
Plaisir d'Amour

Summer
When summer came
My father left the house
He tied a ribbon in his hair

Ardal O'Hanlon is one of Ireland's most acclaimed come-
dians. His role as Father Dougal McGuire in Channel 4's
Father Ted won him the BAFTA for Best Comedy Actor in
1999. His most recent incarnation is that of novelist, with
his first book, *The Talk of the Town*, a bestseller.

And wore a Kaftan dress.
My mother watched him walking down the street
'He'll break his neck in that', she said –
'As if I care'.

He toured the world
And met a guru in Tibet.
'I've slept with women too' he wrote
'And they not half my age'.
My mother threw his letter in the fire –
'The lying ghett – he couldn't climb the stairs
With all his years'.

She burned her bra
And wrote with lipstick on a card –
'I've got two sailors in the house
From Martinique.
They've got your children's eyes'.
My father didn't wait to answer that
He came back home.

And sitting by the fire
He said he'd lied
He'd never slept with anyone but her.
My mother said she'd never lied herself –
She'd thrown the sailors out an hour before he came.
My father's heart would never be the same –
Plaisir d'Amour

Autumn
Through autumn days
My father felt the leaves
Burning in the corners of his mind.
My mother, who was younger by a year,
Looked young and fair.
The sailors from the port of Martinique
Had kissed her cheek.

He searched the house
And hidden in a trunk beneath the bed
My father found his second-hand guitar.
He found her see-through skirt
With matching vest.
'You wore French knickers once' he said
'I liked them best.'

'I gave them all away', my mother cried
'To sailors and to captains of the sea.
I'm not half-dead
I'm fit for any bed – including yours'.
She wore a sailor's cap
And danced around the room
While father strummed his second-hand guitar.

He made the bed
He wore his Kaftan dress
A ribbon in his hair.
'I'll play it one more time,' he said
'And you can sing'.
She sang the only song they knew –
Plaisir d'Amour

Winter
At sixty-four
My mother died
At sixty-five
My father.

Comment from a neighbour
Who was there;
'They'd pass for twenty'.
Plaisir d'Amour

Schoolfriends

SUSAN CONNOLLY

*When I was a young girl I used to seek
pleasure – Nina Simone*

Lost in horse-play
on the school stage,
our high-spirited laughter
rang through the empty hall.
While everyone else 'studied' –
we took turns to play the piano.
One practised handstands
while the other played,
and soon we walked more gracefully
on our hands than on our feet.

Inventing stories of men
peering at us
through the remote piano-room
window, we ran back
along freezing corridors
to a nun
who believed our tale
and gave us
sweetened tea. Slyly
we smiled at our success.

We were the best of friends,
with 'chestnut' hair
and 'hazel' eyes. Such friends
that when we fought
we lashed out with spiky fists
in a burst of uncontrolled rage.
Later, standing by an upstairs
window, I'd feel
the whole of love and hate
well up in me, and press against
my growing frame.

The kind of playfulness
we took for granted
died in me that September
I returned to find you gone.
And though your bitter letters
stung me, I couldn't understand
them
till long after the single pliant
stem we once had been
reached out again
and quietly divided.

The face you and I wore
as young girls
was only a mask of innocence –
but it helped dispel
a darkness in us. And long after
I took off that child-mask
to see what I really looked like,
I heard a young voice within me
– yours and mine –
a voice fresh, innocent and wise.

Ship of Death

KERRY HARDIE

Watching you, for the first time,
turn to prepare your boat, my mother;
making it clear you have other business now –
the business of your future –
I was washed-through with anger.

It was a first survey,
an eye thrown
over sails, oars, timbers,
as many a time I'd seen that practised eye
scan a laden table.

How can you plan going off like this
when we stand at last, close enough, if the wind is right,
to hear what the other is saying?
I never thought you'd do this, turning away,
mid-sentence, your hand testing a rope,

your ear tuned
to the small thunder of the curling wave
on the edge of the great-night sea,
neither regretful nor afraid –
anxious only for the tide.

READ BY OLIVIA O'LEARY

Olivia O'Leary was the first woman to front BBC's
Newsnight and has won numerous awards for her
reporting of current affairs. She has written on politics
for the *Irish Times* and the *Sunday Tribune* and co-wrote
the biography of former Irish President Mary Robinson.

The Boys of Barr na Sráide

SIGERSON CLIFFORD

READ BY
MICHEAL Ó MUIRCHEARTAIGH

O the town it climbs the mountain and looks upon the sea,
And sleeping time or waking 'tis there I long to be,
To walk again that kindly street, the place I grew a man
And the Boys of Barr na Sráide went hunting for the wran.

With cudgels stout we roamed about to hunt the droileen
We looked for birds in every furze from Letter to Dooneen:
We sang for joy beneath the sky, life held no print or plan
And we Boys in Barr na Sráide, hunting for the wran.

And when the hills were bleeding and the rifles were aflame,
To the rebel homes of Kerry the Saxon stranger came,
But the men who dared the Auxies and beat the Black and Tans
Were the Boys of Barr na Sráide hunting for the wran.

And here's a toast to them tonight, the lads who laughed with me,
By the groves of Carhan river or the slopes of Beenatee,
John Dawley and Batt Andy, and the Sheehans Con and Dan,
And the Boys of Barr na Sráide who hunted for the wran.

And now they toil on foreign soil, where they have gone their way
Deep in the heart of London town or over on Broadway.
And I am left to sing their deeds, and praise them while I can
Those Boys of Barr na Sráide who hunted for the wran.

And when the wheel of life runs down and peace comes over me,
O lay me down in that old town between the hills and sea,
I'll take my sleep in those green fields the place my life began,
Where the Boys of Barr na Sráide went hunting for the wran.

Born in Dingle in Co. Kerry, Micheal Ó Muircheartaigh
is the quintessential voice of the GAA. His radio
commentary, delivered in the unmistakeable accent of
a Gaelgeoir, is beloved the land over and his witticisms
are quoted from pub stool to internet site.

The Ballad of Father Gilligan

W B YEATS

The old priest Peter Gilligan
Was weary night and day;
For half his flock were in their beds
Or under green sods lay.

Once, while he nodded on a chair,
At the moth-hour of eve,
Another poor man sent for him,
And he began to grieve.

'I have no rest, nor joy, nor peace,
For people die and die';
And after cried he, 'God forgive!
My body spake, not I!'

He knelt, and leaning on the chair
He prayed and fell asleep;
And the moth-hour went from the
    fields,
And stars began to peep.

They slowly into millions grew,
And leaves shook in the wind;
And God covered the world with
    shade,
And whispered to mankind.

Upon the time of sparrow-chirp
When the moths came once more,
The old priest Peter Gilligan
Stood upright on the floor.

'Mavrone, mavrone! The man has
    died
While I slept on the chair';
He roused his horse out of its sleep
And rode with little care.

He rode now as he never rode,
By rocky lane and fen;
The sick man's wife opened the
    door:
'Father! You come again!'

'And is the poor man dead?' he
    cried.
'He died an hour ago.'
The old priest Peter Gilligan
In grief swayed to and fro.

'When you were gone, he turned
    and died
As merry as a bird.'
The old priest Peter Gilligan
He knelt him at that word.

He Who hath made the night of
    stars
For souls who tire and bleed,
Sent one of His great angels down
To help me in my need.

He Who is wrapped in purple robes,
With planets in His care,
Had pity on the least of things
Asleep upon a chair.'

Milo O'Shea began his acting career as a child in Dublin. He continued his career at the Gate and Abbey theatres before moving on to London's West End and Broadway. He has starred in numerous films, including *Barbarella*, *The Verdict* and *The Butcher Boy*, and TV shows such as *Cheers* and *Frasier*. He recently completed the films *Puckoon* and *Mystics*.

Canticle

JOHN F DEANE

Sometimes when you walk down to the red gate
hearing the scrape-music of your shoes across gravel,
a yellow moon will lift over the hill;
you swing the gate shut and lean on the topmost bar
as if something has been accomplished in the world;
a night wind mistles through the poplar leaves
and all the noise of the universe stills
to an oboe hum, the given note of a perfect
music; there is a vast sky wholly dedicated
to the stars and you know, with certainty,
that all the dead are out, up there, in one
holiday flotilla, and that they celebrate
the fact of a red gate and a yellow moon
that tunes their instruments with you to the symphony.

Morgan O'Sullivan has acted as an executive producer
and co-producer on films such as *Braveheart*, *Angela's
Ashes* and *Veronica Guerin*. Prior to this, he was a
broadcaster with RTE and managed Ardmore Film
Studios.

CeaseFire

MICHAEL LONGLEY

I

Put in mind of his own father and moved to tears
Achilles took him by the hand and pushed the old king
Gently away, but Priam curled up at his feet and
Wept with him until their sadness filled the building.

II

Taking Hector's corpse into his own hands Achilles
Made sure it was washed and, for the old king's sake,
Laid it out in uniform, ready for Priam to carry
Wrapped like a present home to Troy at daybreak.

III

When they had eaten together it pleased them both
To stare at each other's beauty as lovers might,
Achilles built like a god, Priam good-looking still
And full of conversation, who earlier had sighed:

IV

'I get down on my hands and knees and do what must be done
And kiss Achilles' hand, the killer of my son.'

READ BY FINTAN O'TOOLE

Fintan O'Toole is one of Ireland's leading political and
cultural commentators. He has been drama critic for
In-Dublin magazine, *The Sunday Tribune*, the *New York
Daily News* and the *Irish Times*, and Literary Advisor to
the Abbey Theatre. Since 1988 he has been a columnist
for the *Irish Times*.

The Fairies

WILLIAM ALLINGHAM

READ BY MAUREEN POTTER

Up the airy mountain,
Down the rushy glen,
We daren't go a-hunting
For fear of little men;
Wee folk, good folk,
Trooping all together;
Green jacket, red cap,
And white owl's feather!

Down along the rocky shore
Some make their home —
They live on crispy pancakes
Of yellow tide-foam;
Some in the reeds
Of the black mountain lake,
With frogs for their watch-dogs,
All night awake.

High on the hill-top
The old King sits;
He is now so old and grey
He's nigh lost his wits.
With a bridge of white mist
Columbkill he crosses,
On his stately journeys
From Slieveleague to Rosses;
Or going up with music
On cold starry nights
To sup with the Queen
Of the gay Northern Lights.

They stole little Bridget
For seven years long;
When she came down again
Her friends were all gone.
They took her lightly back,
Between the night and morrow;
They thought that she was fast
   asleep,
But she was dead with sorrow.
They have kept her ever since
Deep within the lake,
On a bed of flag-leaves,
Watching till she wake.

By the craggy hill-side,
Through the mosses bare,
They have planted thorn-trees
For pleasure here and there.
Is any man so daring
As dig one up in spite,
He shall find their sharpest thorns
In his bed at night.

Up the airy mountain,
Down the rushy glen,
We daren't go a-hunting
For fear of little men;
Wee folk, good folk,
Trooping all together;
Green jacket, red cap,
And white owl's feather!

Maureen Potter has been described as the queen of Irish comedy appearing in over 50 pantomimes at Dublin's Gaiety Theatre. She starred in her own summer show, *Gaels of Laughter*, for an unbroken run of 18 seasons and has appeared with such Irish theatrical luminaries as Michael MacLiammoir, Cyril Cusack and Siobhan McKenna.

Bewley's Oriental Café, Westmoreland Street

PAUL DURCAN

READ BY DEIRDRE PURCELL

Dublin born, Deirdre Purcell started her eclectic career as a civil servant before joining the Abbey Theatre as an actress. She moved to RTE as a newscaster and then became an award-winning journalist for the *Sunday Tribune*. Since 1990 she has published nine critically acclaimed novels. She adapted her own novel, *Falling for a Dancer*, for BBC TV, while *Love Hate Adore* was shortlisted for the Orange Prize.

When she asked me to keep an eye on her things
I told her I'd be glad to keep an eye on her things.
While she breakdanced off to the ladies' loo
I concentrated on keeping an eye on her things.
What are you doing? – a Security Guard growled,
his moustache gnawing at the beak of his peaked cap.
When I told him that a young woman whom I did not know
Had asked me to keep an eye on her things, he barked:
Instead of keeping an eye on the things
Of a young woman whom you do not know,
Keep an eye on your own things.
I put my two hands on his hips and squeezed him:
Look – for me the equivalent of the Easter Rising
Is to be accosted by a woman whom I do not know
And asked by her to keep an eye on her things;
On her medieval backpack and on her spaceage Walkman;
Calm down and cast aside your peaked cap
And take down your trousers and take off your shoes
And I will keep an eye on your things also.
Do we not cherish all the children of the nation equally?
That woman does not know the joy she has given me
By asking me if I would keep an eye on her things;
I feel as if I am on a Dart to Bray,
Keeping an eye on her things;
More radical than being on the pig's back,
Keeping an eye on nothing.
The security Guard made a heap on the floor
Of his pants and shoes,
Sailing his peaked cap across the café like a frisbee.
His moustache sipped at a glass of milk.
It is as chivalrous as it is transcendental
To be sitting in Bewley's Oriental Café
With a naked Security Guard,
Keeping an eye on his things
And on old ladies
With thousands of loaves of brown bread under their palaeolithic oxters.

Swineherd

EILÉAN NÍ CHUILLEANÁIN

When all this is over, said the swineherd,
I mean to retire, where
Nobody will have heard about my special skills
And conversation is mainly about the weather.

I intend to learn how to make coffee, at least as well
As the Portuguese lay-sister in the kitchen
And polish the brass fenders every day.
I want to lie awake at night
Listening to cream crawling to the top of the jug
And the water lying soft in the cistern.

I want to see an orchard where the trees grow in straight lines
And the yellow fox finds shelter between the navy-blue trunks,
Where it gets dark early in summer
And the apple-blossom is allowed to wither on the bough.

READ BY NIALL QUINN

Soccer star Niall Quinn recently retired after a career
both in the Premiership for Arsenal and Manchester City
and at international level for Ireland. He was awarded an
honorary MBE in recognition of his donation of the
proceeds of his testimonial match to children's charities.
He lives in Co Kildare.

A Disused Shed in Co Wexford

DEREK MAHON

Let them not forget us, the weak among the asphodels — seferis, mythistorema.
Translated by Keeley and Sherrard.

Even now there are places where a thought might grow —
Peruvian mines, worked out and abandoned
To a slow clock of condensation,
An echo trapped for ever, and a flutter
Of wild-flowers in the lift-shaft,
Indian compounds where the wind dances
And a door bangs with diminished confidence,
Lime crevices behind rippling rain-barrels;
Dog corners for bone burials;
And in a disused shed in Co Wexford.

Deep in the grounds of a burnt-out hotel,
Among the bathtubs and the washbasins
A thousand mushrooms crowd to a keyhole.
This is the one star in their firmament
Or frames a star within a star.
What should they do there but desire?
So many days beyond the rhododendrons
With the world waltzing in its bowl of cloud,
They have learnt patience and silence
Listening to the rooks querulous in the high wood.

They have been waiting for us in a foetor
Of vegetable sweat since civil war days,
Since the gravel-crunching, interminable departure
Of the expropriated mycologist.
He never came back, and light since then
Is a keyhole rusting gently after rain.
Spiders have spun, flies dusted to mildew
And once a day, perhaps, they have heard something —
A trickle of masonry, a shout from the blue
Or a lorry changing gear at the end of the lane.

An architect by profession, Ruairi Quinn became a
member of Dublin City Council in 1974 and went on to
become Leader of the Labour Party from 1997 to 2002.
As Labour Leader he oversaw the amalgamation of
Labour with Democratic Left. He served in three coalition
Governments as Minister.

There have been deaths, the pale flesh flaking
Into the earth that nourished it;
And nightmares, born of these and the grim
Dominion of stale air and rank moisture.
Those nearest the door grow strong –
'Elbow room! Elbow room!'
The rest, dim in a twilight of crumbling
Utensils and broken pitchers, groaning
For their deliverance, have been so long
Expectant that there is left only the posture.

A half century, without visitors, in the dark –
Poor preparation for the cracking lock
And creak of hinges, Magi, moonmen,
Powdery prisoners of the old regime,
Web-throated, stalked like triffids, racked by drought
And insomnia, only the ghost of a scream
At the flash-bulb firing-squad we wake them with
Shows there is life yet in their feverish forms.
Grown beyond nature now, soft food for worms,
They lift frail heads in gravity and good faith.

They are begging us, you see, in their wordless way,
To do something, to speak on their behalf
Or at least not to close the door again.
Lost people of Treblinka and Pompeii!
'Save us, save us' they seem to say
'Let the god not abandon us
Who have come so far in darkness and in pain.
We too had our lives to live.
You with your light meter and relaxed itinerary,
Let not our naïve labours have been in vain!'

for J G Farrell

The Did-You-Come-Yets
of the Western World

RITA ANN HIGGINS

READ BY GERRY RYAN

When he says to you:
You look so beautiful
You smell so nice
How I've missed you –
And did you come yet?

It means nothing,
And he is smaller
Than a mouse's fart.

Don't listen to him
Go to Annaghdown Pier
With your father's rod.
Don't necessarily hold out
For the biggest one;
Oftentimes the biggest ones
Are the smallest in the end.

Bring them all home,
But not together.
One by one is the trick;
Avoid red herrings and scandal.

Maybe you could take two
On the shortest day of the year.

Time is the cheater here
Not you, so don't worry.

Many will bite the usual bait;
They will talk their slippery way
Through fine clothes and expensive
Perfume,
Fishing up your independence

These are
The did-you-come-yets of the
    western
World,
The feather and fin rufflers.
Pity for them they have no wisdom.

Others will bite at any bait.
Maggot, suspender, or dead worm.
Throw them to the sharks.

In time one will crawl
Out from under thigh-land.
Although drowning he will say,

'Woman I am terrified, why is this
    house shaking?'

And you'll know he's the one.

Gerry Ryan is best known for his topical talk show
The Gerry Ryan Show. Before this, Gerry worked
on documentaries and current affairs programmes
on RTE Radio 1. He has also presented a wide variety
of programmes including several telethons and the
Eurovision Song Contest. In his current TV show,
Ryan Confidential, he interviews a range of
well-known Irish people.

Peter Street

PETER SIRR

I'd grown almost to love this street
each time I passed looking up
to pin my father's face to a window, feel myself

held in his gaze. Today there's a building site
where the hospital stood and I stop and stare
stupidly at the empty air, looking for him.

I'd almost pray some ache remain
like a flaw in the structure, something unappeasable
waiting in the fabric, between floors, in some

obstinate, secret room. A crane moves
delicately in the sky, in its own language.
Forget all that, I think as I pass, make it

a marvellous house; music should roam the corridors,
joy readily occur, St Valentine's
stubborn heart comes floating from Whitefriar Street

to prevail, to undo injury, to lift my father from his bed,
let him climb down the dull red brick, effortlessly,
and run off with his life in his hands.

READ BY JIM SHERIDAN

Jim Sheridan began his career in Dublin theatre and went
on to co-found the alternative Project Arts group. He
headed to America where he shot to fame with his Oscar-
nominated directorial debut *My Left Foot* which he also
wrote. This was to form a successful partnership with the
actor Daniel Day Lewis that went on to yield such films as
In the Name of the Father and *The Boxer*

A Drover

PADRAIC COLUM

To Meath of the pastures,
　From wet hills by the sea,
Through Leitrim and Longford
　Go my cattle and me.

I hear in the darkness
　Their slipping and breathing.
I name them the bye-ways
　They're to pass without heeding.

Then the wet, winding roads,
　Brown bogs with black water;
And my thoughts on white ships
　And the King o' Spain's daughter.

O farmer, strong farmer!
　You can spend at the fair,
But your face you must turn
　To your crops and your care.

And soldiers, red soldiers!
　You've seen many lands;
But you walk two and two,
　And by captain's commands.

O the smell of the beasts,
　The wet wind in the morn,
And the proud and hard earth
　Never broken for corn!

And the crowds at the fair,
　The herds loosened and blind,
Loud words and dark faces
　And the wild blood behind.

(O strong men with your best
　I would strive breast to breast
I could quiet your herds
　With my words, with my words!)

I will bring you, my kine,
　Where there's grass to the knee;
But you'll think of scant croppings
　Harsh with salt of the sea.

Dick Spring left politics in 2002 after 21 years, having helped the Labour Party back into Government, and playing a pivotal role in the Good Friday Agreement. He led the Labour Party from 1982 to 1997 and served as Tanaiste in three coalition Governments .

Everything Is Going To Be All Right

DEREK MAHON

How should I not be glad to contemplate
the clouds clearing beyond the dormer window
and a high tide reflected on the ceiling?
There will be dying, there will be dying,
but there is no need to go into that.
The poems flow from the hand unbidden
and the hidden source is the watchful heart.
The sun rises in spite of everything
and the far cities are beautiful and bright.
I lie here in a riot of sunlight
watching the day break and the clouds flying.
Everything is going to be all right.

Niall Toibin has been in show business since 1948,
performing in theatre, variety, cabaret, radio, TV and
film. He starred in the Tony award-winning production of
Brendan Behan's *Borstal Boy*, and is a familiar face on
British and Irish TV from series such as *Bracken*, *The Irish
RM* and *Minder*.

I See His Blood Upon the Rose

JOSEPH MARY PLUNKETT

READ BY SILE DE VALERA

I see His blood upon the rose
And in the stars the glory of His eyes,
His body gleams amid eternal snows,
His tears fall from the skies.

I see his face in every flower;
The thunder and the singing of the birds
Are but His voice – and carven by His power
Rocks are His written words.

All pathways by His feet are worn,
His strong heart stirs the ever-beating sea,
His crown of thorns is twined with every thorn,
His cross is every tree.

Sile de Valera is granddaughter of Eamon de Valera
and has followed in his footsteps as a politician and
member of Fianna Fail. She has been a Dail deputy for
Clare since 1987 and served as Minister of Arts,
Heritage, Gaeltacht and the Islands from 1997 to 2002.
She is now Minister at the Department of Education
and Science.

Ted Walsh is a race horse trainer and TV pundit. As a jockey, Walsh won the Champion Amateur Jockey title a record 11 times before turning professional. He has gone on to become a successful trainer, running a family based training yard in Kill, Co Kildare. With his son, jockey Ruby Walsh, he achieved a unique feat in horseracing when Papillon won the Aintree Grand National in 2000. Ted was the trainer and Ruby was the jockey. Ted has now a successful career as a horseracing commentator and pundit, regularly working for RTE television and the UK's Channel 4.

The Aluminium Box

FRANK ORMSBY

It demands to be handled with care,
has a seat to itself on the bus from Enniskillen.
John Wayne is in it and Clint Walker and Joel McCrea
and Randolph Scott who never lost his hat,
Witchita and Dodge City and Boothill.
Strongbox, capsule, payload, portable safe,
with all of us riding shotgun.

A big-arsed countrywoman sits on it once,
reversing in oblivious. We watch her leap
as though bitten by a rattlesnake.
Steve Reeves is in it and Red Buttons and Rip Torn,
its sealed stillness holding the light at bay
between sleepy, no-horse towns.
'Kirk' and 'Burt', we mutter, like bilious frogs.

A couple of nights at the Astral,
two at the Ritz. Next stop the Adelphi
Marilyn is in it and Gina and Sophia Loren,
the saloon girls of El Paso and Santa Fe
with skirts at the ready.
Open-mouthed, we will yearn through smoky air
for the lips of Kim Novak and Tuesday Weld.

Getting off a mile from the town
is like leaving the stalls before the trailers finish.
'Big crowd on the bus, son?' my mother drawls,
her habitual question.
'It was packed, Maw,' I tell her, 'packed to the door.'

Beannacht

JOHN O'DONOGHUE

On the day when
the weight deadens
on your shoulders
and you stumble,
may the clay dance
to balance you.

And when your eyes
freeze behind
the grey window
and the ghost of loss
gets in to you,
may a flock of colours,
indigo, red, green
and azure blue
come to awaken in you
a meadow of delight.

When the canvas frays
in the currach of thought
and a stain of ocean
blackens beneath you,
may there come across the waters
a path of yellow moonlight
to bring you safely home.

May the nourishment of the earth
be yours,
may the clarity of light be yours,
may the fluency of the ocean be
yours,
may the protection of the ancestors
be yours.

And so may a slow
wind work these words
of love around you,
an invisible cloak
to mind your life.

for Josie, my mother

Kathleen Watkins started her career as a singer and
harpist, and later joined RTE as an announcer. She is
married to broadcaster Gay Byrne. She also served for
ten years as a member of the Arts Council.

Anseo

PAUL MULDOON

Bill Whelan, Grammy award-winning composer of *Riverdance: The Show*, has worked extensively in theatre, television and film. His work in international film includes *Lamb*, which he co-composed with Van Morrison; his score for the Jim Sheridan/Terry George film, *Some Mother's Son*; and the original score for the adaptation of Brian Friel's *Dancing at Lughnasa* which starred Meryl Streep.

When the Master was calling the
    roll
At the primary school in
    Collegelands,
You were meant to call back *Anseo*
And raise your hand
As your name occurred.
Anseo, meaning here, here and now,
All present and correct,
Was the first word of Irish I spoke.
The last name on the ledger
Belonged to Joseph Mary Plunkett
    Ward
And was followed, as often as not,
By silence, knowing looks,
A nod and a wink, the Master's droll
'And where's our little Ward-of-
    court?'

I remember the first time he came
    back
The Master had sent him out
Along the hedges
To weigh up for himself and cut
A stick with which he would be
    beaten.
After a while, nothing was spoken;
He would arrive as a matter of
    course
With an ash-plant, a salley-rod.
Or, finally, the hazel-wand
He had whittled down to a whip-
    lash,

Its twist of red and yellow lacquers
Sanded and polished,
And altogether so delicately
    wrought
That he had engraved his initials on
    it.

I last met Joseph Mary Plunkett
    Ward
In a pub just over the Irish border.
He was living in the open,
In a secret camp
On the other side of the mountain.
He was fighting for Ireland,
Making things happen.
And he told me, Joe Ward,
Of how he had risen through the
    ranks
To Quartermaster, Commandant:
How every morning at parade
His volunteers would call back *Anseo*
And raise their hands
As their names occurred.

The Planter's Daughter

AUSTIN CLARKE

When night stirred at sea
And the fire brought a crowd in,
They say that her beauty
Was music in mouth
And few in the candlelight
Thought her too proud,
For the house of the planter
Is known by the trees.

Men that had seen her
Drank deep and were silent,
The women were speaking
Wherever she went –
As a bell that is rung
Or a wonder told shyly.
And O she was the Sunday
In every week.

READ BY TERRY WOGAN

Terry Wogan moved from RTE radio to the BBC early in his career and presented regular shows on Radio 1 and Radio 2. His extensive TV credits include his live chat show series *Wogan* which he presented for seven years on BBC 1, and he has presented numerous other shows, including the *Eurovision Song Contest*. Terry was awarded an honorary OBE in 1997.

Poetry Acknowledgements

The publishers would like to acknowledge the following for permission to reproduce copyright material. Every effort has been made to trace the copyright holders of the material contained in this book but in some instances this has not proved to be possible. In the event that the publishers are contacted by any of the untraceable copyright holders after publication of this book, the publishers shall endeavour to rectify the position accordingly as soon as reasonably practicable.

The poems included in this collection have been reproduced by the kind permission of their authors, or are exempt from copyright, unless otherwise stated below.

2. A Glass of Beer – James Stephens. Reproduced by permission of The Society of Authors as the Literary Representative of the Estate of James Stephens.

6, 8, 95, 101. 'Nuala', 'God's Laughter', 'A Kind of Trust' and 'Poem From a Three Year Old' by Brendan Kennelly. Reproduced by permission of Bloodaxe.

7, 19, 24, 58, 70, 108. 'The Second Coming', 'Never Give All the Heart', 'The Fisherman', 'What Then?', 'The Fiddler of Dooney' and 'The Ballad of Father Gilligan' by W B Yeats. Reproduced with permission of AP Watt Ltd on behalf of Michael B Yeats.

10. 'Four Voices Without an Instrument' by Medbh McGuckian. Reproduced by permission of The Gallery Press.

11. 'Father and Son' by F R Higgins. Reproduced by the kind permission of Ruth Dodd.

12, 38, 62, 64, 71. 'A Christmas Childhood', 'I Grabbed an Education', excerpted lines from The Paddiad or The Devil as a Patron of Irish Letters, 'Stony Grey Soil' and 'To A Child' by Patrick Kavanagh. Reprinted by permission of the Trustees of the Estate of the late Katherine B Kavanagh through the Jonathan Williams Literary Agency.

16, 45, 67, 81. 'Mid-term Break', 'The Rain Stick', 'The Singer's House' and 'Requiem for the Croppies' from Opened Ground Poems 1966–1996 by Seamus Heaney published by Faber & Faber. Reproduced with the permission of Faber & Faber.

18. 'The Friction of Feet in Time' by Michael Coady. Reproduced with permission of The Gallery Press.

25, 51, 118. 'An Old Woman of the Roads', 'She Moved Through the Fair' and 'The Drover' by Padraic Colum. Reproduced with permission of the Estate of Padraic Colum.

26. 'Shades of Ranelagh' by Macdara Woods. Reproduced with permission of The Dedalus Press.

27. 'The Christmas Rose' by C. Day Lewis from The Complete Poems, published by Sinclair-Stevenson 1992, copyright © 1992 in this edition, and the Estate of C. Day Lewis. Reproduced with the permission of The Random House Group Ltd.

28, 123. 'Duffy's Circus' and 'Anseo' by Paul Muldoon from Poems 1968–1998, published by Faber and Faber. Reproduced with the permission of Faber & Faber.

30. 'Winter Birds' by Moya Cannon. Reproduced by permission of The Gallery Press.

31. 'Death of an Irishwoman' by Michael Hartnett. Reproduced by permission of The Gallery Press.

32. 'Nude' by Nuala Ni Dhomhnaill (translated by Paul Muldoon). Reproduced by permission of The Gallery Press.

36. 'Someone' by Dennis O'Driscoll from Hidden Extras, published by Anvil Press Poetry 1987. Reproduced with the permission of Anvil Press Poetry.

40. 'July in Bettystown' by Gerard Fanning. Reproduced with the permission of The Dedalus Press.

42. 'Night Feed' by Eavan Boland. Reproduced with the permission of Carcanet Press Ltd.

46, 78. 'Bagpipe Music' and 'The Sunlight on the Garden' from Collected Poems published by Faber & Faber. Reproduced by permission of David Higham Associates.

52. 'Seals at High Island' by Richard Murphy. Reproduced by permission of The Gallery Press.

54. 'Sunday's Well' by Vona Groarke. Reproduced by permission of The Gallery Press.

55. 'Christy Brown Came to Town' by Richard Harris. Reproduced by permission of Noel Harris.

57. 'How to Be My Heart' by Pat Boran from *The Shape of Water*, 1996, copyright Pat Boran/The Dedalus Press, all rights granted.

61. 'Claudy' by James Simmons. Reproduced by permission of The Gallery Press.

65. 'Ulster Names' by John Hewitt from *The Collected Poems of John Hewitt*, edited by Frank Ormsby (Blackstaff Press, 1991). Reprinted by permission of Blackstaff Press on behalf of the Estate of John Hewitt.

73, 87, 114, 119. 'Shapes and Shadows', 'Antarctica', 'A Disused Shed in Co Wexford' and 'Everything is Going To Be All Right' by Derek Mahon. Reproduced by permission of The Gallery Press.

74. 'Thems Your Mammy's Pills' by Leland Bardwell. Reproduced by permission of The Dedalus Press.

76. 'Ómós do John Millington Synge' by Máirtin Ó Direáin. Reproduced by permission of Stiofán Ó hAnnracháin.

77, 82. 'There Are Days' and 'The Country Fiddler' by John Montague. Reproduced by permission of The Gallery Press.

84. 'Literary History' by Rita Kelly from *Travelling West* published by Arlen House, 2000. Reproduced by permission of Rita Kelly.

88. 'The People I Grew Up With Were Afraid' by Michael Gorman. Reproduced by permission of Salmon Publishers and Michael Gorman.

90. 'Solstice' by Gerry Dawe. Reproduced by permission of The Gallery Press.

94. 'The View From Under the Table' by Paula Meehan. Reproduced by permission of Carcanet Press Ltd.

96. 'The Jackeen's Lament for the Blasket' by Brendan Behan (translated by Donagh MacDonagh). Reproduced by permission of The Sayle Agency.

97. 'A Woman Untouched' by Frank McGuinness. Reproduced by permission of The Gallery Press.

105. 'Schoolfriends' by Susan Connolly. Reproduced by permission of The Dedalus Press.

106. 'Ship of Death' by Kerry Hardie. Reproduced by permission of The Gallery Press.

107. 'The Boys of Barr na Sráide' by Sigerson Clifford. Copyright © The Estate of Sigerson Clifford 1986. Reprinted by permission of Mercier Press Ltd, Cork.

109. 'Canticle' by John F Deane. Reproduced by permission of The Dedalus Press.

113. 'Swineherd' by Eiléan Ní Chuilleanán. Reproduced by permission of The Gallery Press.

116. 'The Did-You-Come-Yets of the Western World' by Rita Ann Higgins. Reproduced by permission of Bloodaxe Ltd and Rita Ann Higgins.

117. 'Peter Street' by Peter Sirr. Reproduced by permission of The Gallery Press.

121. 'The Aluminium Box' by Frank Ormsby. Reproduced by permission of The Gallery Press.

124. 'The Planter's Daughter' by Austin Clarke. Reproduced by permission of R Dardis Clarke, 17 Oscar Square, Dublin.

Photo credits

Bertie Ahern – courtesy of Bertie Ahern
Robert Ballagh © Derek Speirs
Patrick Bergin © Michael Tighe
Maeve Binchy © The Orion Publishing Group
Charlie Bird © Lensmen
Tara Blaze © Barry McCall
Luka Bloom © Amelia Stein
Bono © Anton Corbijn
John Bowman © RTÉ Stills
Paul Brady © Nick Haddow
Pierce Brosnan © Greg Gorman
Vincent Browne – courtesy of Vincent Browne
Gabriel Byrne © Roberto Dutesco
Gay Byrne © RTÉ Picture Archive
Liam Clancy – courtesy of Liam Clancy
Paddy Cole © Priory Studios
Andrea Corr © Kevin Westenberg
Sharon Corr © Kevin Westenberg
Phil Coulter © Colm Henry
John Creedon © RTÉ Stills
Anthony Cronin © Tony Gavin, *Sunday Independent*
Jeananne Crowley – courtesy of Jeananne Crowley
Bill Cullen – courtesy of Bill Cullen
Dana – courtesy of Dana
Ian Dempsey © Mark McCall
Dermot Desmond – courtesy of Dermot Desmond
Moya Doherty © Mark McCall
Theo Dorgan – courtesy of Theo Dorgan

Anne Doyle – courtesy of Anne Doyle
Danny Doyle © Robin Reid Photography
Ronnie Drew – courtesy of Ronnie Drew
Joe Duffy © RTÉ Stills Dept
Myles Dungan © courtesy of Myles Dungan
Eamon Dunphy © Mark McCall
Paul Durcan © Hugh McElveen
Dave Fanning – courtesy of Dave Fanning
Colin Farrell – courtesy of Colin Farrell
Marian Finucane – courtesy of Marian Finucane
Brenda Fricker – courtesy of Cassie Mayer Ltd
Gavin Friday © Mary Scanlon
James Galway © Hanya Chlala c/o Arena Images
Bob Geldof © Colm Henry
Des Geraghty – courtesy of Des Geraghty
Brendan Gleeson – courtesy of Brendan Gleeson
Larry Gogan – courtesy of Larry Gogan
Adrian Hardiman © Collins Photo Agency
Mary Harney © MacInnes
Richard Harris © Colm Henry
Shay Healy © Greg French
Seamus Heaney © Norman MacBeath
Michael D Higgins – courtesy of Michael D Higgins
John Hume – courtesy of John Hume
Neil Jordan – courtesy of Neil Jordan
Fergal Keane © Leon Farrell/Photocall Ireland

Frank Kelly © Brendan Harrington
Gerry Kelly © Jill Jennings, Christopher Hill
John Kelly © Shane McCarthy
Brian Kennedy © Allessandro Cecchini
Senator Edward M Kennedy – courtesy of the office of Senator Edward M Kennedy
Sister Stanislaus Kennedy – courtesy of Sister Stanislaus Kennedy
Brendan Kennelly – courtesy of Brendan Kennelly
Pat Kenny – courtesy of Pat Kenny
Marian Keyes © Mark McCall
Mick Lally © Joe O'Shaughnessy
Desmond Lynam © Brian Aris
John Lynch © Brian Moody
Ciaran MacMathuna – courtesy of Ciaran MacMathuna
Jimmy Magee © Val Sheehan, *Sunday World*
Tommy Makem © J Sylvester
Paddy Moloney – courtesy of Paddy Moloney
Eamon McCann © Colm Henry
Charlie McCreevy – courtesy of Charlie McCreevy
Paul McGrath© Pat Egan
Paul McGuinness © Mark McCall
Pauline McLynn © Shane McCarthy
Van Morrison © Paul Cox
Mike Murphy – courtesy of Mike Murphy
Kevin Myers – courtesy of Kevin Myers

Christina Noble – courtesy of Christina Noble

Michael Noonan © Peter Kavanagh

Senator David Norris – courtesy of Senator David Norris

Miriam O'Callaghan © RTÉ Stills

Sinead O'Connor © Jim Fitzpatrick

Daniel O'Donnell – courtesy of Daniel O'Donnell

Ardal O'Hanlon © David Schienmann

Deirdre O'Kane © Paul McCarthy

Olivia O'Leary © Colm Henry

Micheal Ó Muircheartaigh © Kinane Studio

Milo O'Shea © James Shannon

Morgan O'Sullivan © Jonathan Hession

Fintan O'Toole © *Irish Times*

Maureen Potter – courtesy of Maureen Potter

Deirdre Purcell © Colm Henry

Niall Quinn © Ray McManus, Sportsfile

Ruairi Quinn – courtesy of Ruairi Quinn

Gerry Ryan – courtesy of Gerry Ryan

Jim Sheridan – Amelia Stein

Dick Spring – Frank Fennell

Niall Toibin – Des Lacey

Sile de Valera – courtesy of Sile de Valera

Ted Walsh © Peter Mooney

Kathleen Watkins – courtesy of Kathleen Watkins

Bill Whelan © Colm Henry

Terry Wogan © BBC Radio 2

Poet biographies

WILLIAM ALLINGHAM (1824–1889)

Born in Ballyshannon, Co Donegal, Allingham was a frequent visitor to London as a young man where he became friendly with the poet Alfred Lord Tennyson. In 1850, he published his first volume of poetry which was followed by several others as well as the long poem *Laurence Bloomfield in Ireland*, largely regarded as his most important work. He married in 1874 and published several more volumes of poetry before his death fifteen years later.

AMERGIN (DATES UNKNOWN)

Amergin was a Milesian prince or druid who settled in Ireland hundreds of years before Christ and is from the *Leabhar Gabhala* or *Book of Invasions*. He is considered one of Ireland's earliest poets and his poem 'The Mystery' is attributed as the first Irish poem.

LELAND BARDWELL (1928–)

Born in India of Irish parents, Bardwell was brought to Ireland at the age of two. Her collections of poetry are *The Mad Cyclist*, *The Fly and the Bedbug,Dostoevsky's Grave*, *New and Selected Poems*, and *The White Beach, New & Selected Poems 1960–1988*. Her novels are *Girl on a Bicycle*, *That London Winter*, *The House*, *There We Have Been* and *Mother to a Stranger*. Her plays include *Thursday* and *Open–Ended Prescription*. She has also broadcast radio plays, including *The Revenge of Constance* and *Just Another Killing*. Her musical, *Edith Piaf*, also toured Ireland. She lives in Co Sligo.

BRENDAN BEHAN (1923-1964)

Author and revolutionary, Behan was in and out of prison for most of his life for his activities with the Irish Republican Army, but became an internationally acclaimed writer and poet. He is the author of autobiographical works such as *Borstal Boy* and *Confessions of an Irish Rebel*.

EAVAN BOLAND (1944–)

Born in Dublin, where she still lives, Boland has published several collections of poetry including *The War Horse*, *In Her Own Image*, *Night Feed*, *The Journey*, *Selected Poems*, *Outside History*, *An Origin Like Water – Collected Poems 1967–1987* and *The Lost Land*. Her recent collections are *A Lost Land* and *Code*. A collection of prose writings, *Object Lessons*, was published in 1995, and with Mark Strand she has edited *The Making of a Poem* and *A Norton Anthology of Poetic Forms*.

PAT BORAN (1963–)

Born in Portlaoise, Boran's poetry collections are *The Unwound Clock*, which won the Patrick Kavanagh Award, *Familiar Things*, *The Shape of Water* and *As the Hand, the Glove*. He has also published a collection of short stories, *Strange Bedfellows*, and short fiction for children, *All the Way to China*, as well as *A Short History of Dublin*. He lives in Dublin.

JOSEPH CAMPBELL (1879–1944)

Born in Belfast, Campbell's interest in folklore and music propelled him to write poetry and songs set to folk tunes, such as his most famous work, 'My Lagan Love'. He was a founder member of the Ulster Literary Theatre. He emigrated to the United States in 1925 and introduced Irish Studies for the first time to the American education system as Lecturer at Fordham University. He returned to Wicklow in 1938 where he lived until his death.

MOYA CANNON

Born in Dunfanaghy, Co Donegal, Cannon is a former editor of the *Poetry Ireland Review*. Her first collection of poetry, *Oar*, for which she received the Brendan Behan Memorial Prize, was published in 1990. Her second collection, *The Parchment Boat*, was published in 1997. She lives in Galway.

EILÉAN NÍ CHUILLEANÁN (1942–)

Born in Cork, ní Chuilleanán has published eight collections of poetry: *Acts and Monuments*, *Site of Ambush*, *Cork*, *The Second Voyage*, *The Rose Geranium*, *The Magdalene Sermon*, *The Brazen Serpent* and *The Girl Who Married the Reindeer*. She won the Patrick Kavanagh Award for *Acts and Monuments* in 1973, and *The Magdalene Sermon* was shortlisted for the *Irish Times*-Aer Lingus Award in 1990, and nominated for the European Literature Prize in 1992. The Irish-American Cultural Institute awarded her the O'Shaughnessy Prize for Poetry in 1992. She lives in Dublin.

AUSTIN CLARKE (1896–1974)

Born in Dublin, Clarke's collections include *Collected Poems*, *Later Poems*, *Flight to Africa and Other Poems*, *Mnemosyne Lay in Dust*, *Old Fashioned Pilgrimage and Other Poems* and *The Echo at Coole and Other Poems*. He wrote many verse plays, including *The Son of Learning*, *The Flame*, *Sister Eucharia*, *Black Fast*, *The Kiss*, *As The Crow Flies*, *The Plot is Ready*, *The Viscount of Blarney*, *The Second Kiss*, *The Plot Succeeds* and *The Moment Next to Nothing*. Most of these were performed by the Dublin Verse-Speaking Society, founded by Clarke and the poet Robert Farren in 1938, and the Lyric Theatre Company, and were published in one volume as *Collected Plays*. He died in Dublin in 1974.

SIGERSON CLIFFORD (1913–1984)

Although born in Cork, Clifford was regarded as a native of Cahersiveen where his family relocated. His father was a tailor in Top Street, Cahersiveen, the location of his famous song, 'The Boys of Barr na Sráide'. He recorded the main events of his life in verse, later collected in *Ballads of a Bogman*.

MICHAEL COADY (1939–)

Born in Carrick-on-Suir, Co Tipperary, Coady's poetry collections are *Two for a Woman, Three for a Man*, *Oven Lane* and *All Souls*, an illustrated compendium of poetry and prose. He has also written short stories for radio, for which he won the the Francis MacManus prize on two occasions. He won the Patrick Kavanagh Award for poetry in 1979. He still lives in Carrick-on-Suir.

PADRAIC COLUM (1881–1972)

Born in Longford, Colum married the writer Mary Molly Gunning Maguire in 1912 and emigrated to New York two years later. Though better known for his later work in other fields, his contributions to the early Irish Dramatic Movement were important and included *Broken Sail*, *The Fiddler's House* and *The Land*. He achieved significant recognition away from the theatre as a poet, novelist, essayist and children's author. Colum and his wife taught Comparative Literature at Columbia University from 1939 to 1956 and in 1958 Columbia honoured him with a doctorate.

SUSAN CONNOLLY (1956–)

Born in Drogheda, Co Louth, where she still lives, Connolly's principal work includes *For the Stranger and Stone*, *Tree Sheltering Water: An Exploration of Sacred and Secular Wells in Co Louth*, *How High the Moon*, *Race to the Sea* and *A Salmon in the Pool*. She was awarded the Patrick and Katherine Kavanagh Fellowship in Poetry in 2001.

GERRY CORR (1933–)

Born in Dundalk, Co Louth, Corr's great interests are music and literature. In his poetry opposites are kin as he blends tragedy and humour in a unique but necessary vision of life. He is the father of the family pop group The Corrs.

ANTHONY CRONIN (1928–)

Born in Co Wexford, Cronin's many works include the novels *The Life of Riley* and *Identity Papers*, several collections of poems including *Poems*; *Collected Poems 1950–73*, *Reductionist Poem*, *41 Sonnet Poems*, *RMS Titanic*, *New and Selected Poems*, *The End of the Modern World*, *Relationships* and *Minotaur*. His non-fiction includes *Dead as Doornails*; *Heritage Now*, *A Question of Modernity*, *An Irish Eye*, *Art for the People?*, *No Laughing Matter: The Life and Times of Flann O' Brien* and *Samuel Beckett: The Last Modernist*. He has edited *New Poems* and *The Courtship of Phelim O'Toole, Stories by William Carleton*. He is a founding member of Aosdána and lives in Dublin.

THOMAS DAVIS (1814–1845)

Born in Mallow in Co Cork, Davis was a poet and balladeer, as well as a chief organiser of the nationalist movement known as 'Young Ireland' and the main contributor to its newspaper, *The Nation*. In 1840 he made a famous speech calling for studies of Irish history at Trinity College, where he had studied law, and was a firm believer in the importance of the Irish language. He wrote many famous ballads such as 'A Nation Once Again' and 'The West's Asleep'. He died in 1845 of fever.

GERRY DAWE (1952–)

Born in Belfast, Dawe is a lecturer at University College Galway and Trinity College Dublin. His poetry includes *Sheltering Places*, *The Lundys Letter* and *Lake Geneva*, and he has also edited *The Younger Irish Poets* and *Across the Roaring Hill: The Protestant Imagination in Modern Ireland*. His criticism includes *How's the Poetry Going*, *False Faces*, and *Against Piety: Essays in Irish Poetry*.

JOHN F DEANE (1943–)

Born in Co Mayo, Deane founded Poetry Ireland and the *Poetry Ireland Review* in 1979. He is also the founding and current editor of the Dedalus Press. He won the O'Shaughnessy Award for Irish Poetry in 1998, and in 2000 the Grand International Prize for Poetry. His poetry collections include *Stalking After Time*, *Winter in Meath*, *Walking On Water* and, most recently, *Manhandling the Deity*. He has also written a collection of short stories, *Free Range*, and two novels, *One Man's Place* and *Undertow*.

NUALA NÍ DHOMHNAILL (1952–)

Born in Lancashire of Irish parents and brought up in the Dingle Gaeltacht and in Nenagh, Co Tipperary, Dhomnaill's collections include *An Dealg Droighin*, *Féar Suaithinseach*, *Rogha Dánta/Selected Poems*, *Pharoh's Daughter* and *Feis*. She has also written plays for children including *Jimín* and *An Ollphiast Ghrána*. Her awards include Duais Sheáin Uí Ríordáin, Gradam an Oireachtas, Duais Na Chomhairle Ealaíne um Filíochta, The Irish American

Foundation Award and the American Ireland Fund Literature Prize. She now lives in Co Dublin.

MÁIRTÍN Ó DÍREÁIN (1910–1988)

Born on the Aran Islands, Ó Díreáin worked as a civil servant for much of his life. His main works include the poetry collections *Rogha Dánta*, *Ó Mórna agus Dánta Eile*, *Ar Ré Dhearóil*, *Cloch Choirnéil*, *Crainn is Cairde*, *Ceacht an Éin*, *Dánta 1939-79*, *Béasa an Túir*, *Tacar Dánta/Selected Poems* and *Craobhóg: Dán*. His autobiographical essays are collected as *Feamainn Bhealtine*. His awards include the An Chomhairle Ealaíon/The Arts Council Awards, the Butler Prize (with Eoghan Ó Tuairisc) and the Ossian Prize for Poetry.

THEO DORGAN (1953–)

Born in Cork, Dorgan's poetry collections are *The Ordinary House of Love*, *Rosa Mundi* and *Sappho's Daughter*. He has also published a selection of poems in Italian, *La Case ai Margini del Mundo*. He has edited *The Great Book of Ireland* (with Gene Lambert), *Revising the Rising* (with Máirín Ní Dhonnachadha, *Irish Poetry Since Kavanagh*, and *Watching the River Flow* (with Noel Duffy). A former Director of Poetry Ireland, he has worked extensively as a broadcaster of literary programmes on both radio and television, and hosts the RTÉ TV books programme *Imprint*. Among his awards are the Listowel Prize for Poetry. He lives in Dublin.

PAUL DURCAN (1944–)

Born in Dublin, where he still lives, Durcan won the Patrick Kavanagh Award in 1974 and the Whitbread Prize for *Daddy, Daddy* in 1990. His books include *Endsville* (with Brian Lynch), *O Westport in the Light of Asia Minor*, *Sam's Cross*, *Teresa's Bar*, *Jesus, Break his Fall*, *Ark of the North*, *The Selected Paul Durcan* (edited by Edna Longley), *Jumping the Train Tracks with Angela*, *The Berlin Wall Café*, *Going Home to Russia*, *In the Land of Punt* (with Gene Lambert), *Jesus and Angela*, *Daddy, Daddy*, *Crazy About Women*, *A Snail in My Prime*, *Give Me Your Hand*, *Christmas Day*; *Greetings to Our Friends in Brazil* and *Cries of an Irish Caveman*.

GERARD FANNING (1952–)

Born in Dublin, Fanning's poetry collections are *Easter Snow*, and *Working for the Government*. He lives in Dublin.

PADRAIC FIACC (1924–)

Born in Belfast, Fiacc emigrated with his family to New York, but he returned to Belfast in 1946. His collections include *Woe to the Boy*, *By the Black Stream*, *Odour of Blood*, *Nights in the Bad Place*, *The Selected Padraic Fiacc*, *Missa Terriblis*, *Ruined Pages*, *Semper vacare* and *Red Earth*. He has also edited *The Wearing of the Black*. His awards include the AE Memorial Award, a major bursary from The Arts Council of Northern Ireland and a Poetry Ireland Award. He lives in Belfast.

GABRIEL FITZMAURICE (1952–)

Born in Moyvane, Co Kerry, where he still lives, Fitzmaurice was Chairman and Literary Advisor of Writer's Week, Listowel, and has published several poetry collections, including *Rainsong*, *Road To The Horizon*, *Dancing Through*, *The Father's Part* and *The Village Sings*. He has also published a collection in Irish entitled *Nocht* and a collection of children's verse, *The Moving Stair*. An award-winner at the Gerard Manley Hopkins Centenary Poetry Competition, he has broadcast extensively on Irish radio and television and has twice represented Ireland at the European Festival of Poetry.

PATRICK GALVIN (1927–)

Born in Cork, Galvin's poetry collections include *Heart of Grace*, *Christ in London*, *The Wood-burners*, *Man on the Porch*, *Madwoman of Cork* and *Folktales for the General*. His plays include *And Him Stretched*, *Cry the Believers*, *Nightfall to Belfast*, *The Last Burning*, *We Do It for Love*, *The Devil's Own People* and *My Silver Bird*. His radio plays include *City Child Come Tailing Home*, *Wolfe*, *Class of '39* and *Quartet for Nightown*. He has published two separate volumes of autobiography: *Song for a Poor Boy* and *Song for a Raggy Boy*. The third part, *Song for a Fly Boy*, is published with the first two as *The Raggy Boy Trilogy*. *Song for a Raggy Boy* has been made into a film starring Aidan Quinn.

RORY GLEESON

Rory is the youngest of the poets featured in this collection at just 13. His father, Brendan, reads his poem 'Emotion', which he wrote for his English class.

OLIVER GOLDSMITH (1728–1774)

Poet, dramatist and essayist, Oliver Goldsmith was born either in Pallas, County Longford or Elphin, Roscommon. He had a severe attack of smallpox at the age of eight which left him badly disfigured for life. In 1744 he went to Trinity College Dublin, ran away in 1746, but returned to graduate in 1749. Instead of pursuing his proposed career in medicine, he travelled throughout Europe, from which experiences he drew on in *The Vicar of Wakefield*. In 1756 he returned destitute to London and drifted into the profession of hack writer for the *Monthly Review*. In 1759 he published his first substantial work. His plays, particularly *She Stoops to Conquer*, became immensely popular and he was celebrated within literary circles, although died leaving huge debts in 1774.

MICHAEL GORMAN (1960–)

Born in Dublin, Gorman is a poet writing in English, Irish and Scottish Gaelic. His collections include *Fax and other Poems*, *Cúis-Ghaoil*, *Bealach Garbh*, *Air a ' Charbad fo Thalamh / On the Underground*, *Faoi Shlí Cualann*, *Gun Urra* and *Up She Flew*.

VONA GROARKE (1964–)

Born in Edgeworthstown, Co Longford, Groarke grew up on a farm outside Athlone. Her collections are *Shale*, *Other People's Houses* and *Flight*. Among her awards are the *Sunday Tribune* New Irish Writer of the Year Award and the Hennessey Cognac Award for Poetry. She lives Co Louth.

KERRY HARDIE (1951–)

Born in Singapore, Hardie grew up in Co Down. Her poetry collections include *A Furious Place* and *Cry for the Hot Belly*, and she has also published two novels, *A Winter Marriage* and *Hannie Bennet*. She was joint winner of the Hennessey Award for Poetry in 1995, and in 1996 she won the UK National Poetry Award. She lives in Co Kilkenny.

RICHARD HARRIS (1930–2002)

Born in Limerick, Harris became a Hollywood superstar and built a film career that lasted six decades. His many memorable performances range from *The Sporting Life* in 1963 to *Unforgiven* in 1992 and *Gladiator* in 2000. As famous for his off-screen antics as his acting, Harris also loved literature and poetry.

MICHAEL HARTNETT (1944–1999)

Born in Co Limerick, Hartnett lived in Dublin for many years. His collections include *Anatomy of a Cliché*, *The Old Hag of Beare*, *Tao*, *Gypsy Ballads*, *A Farewell to English*, *Prisoners*, *Adharca Broic*, *An Phurgóid*, *Do Nuala: Foighne Chrainn*, *Inchichore Haiku*, *Ó Bruadair*, *Selected Poems of Dáibhí Ó Bruadair; A Necklace of Wrens*, *Poems to Younger Women*, *Dánta Naomh Eoin na Croise*, *The Killing of Dreams*, *Haicéad* and *Ó Rathaille The Poems of Aodhaghán Ó Rathaille*. He translated the *Selected Poems of Nuala Ní Dhomhnaill*, co-wrote a play, *An Lasair Choille*, with Caitlín Maude and was co-editor, with James Liddy and Liam O'Connor, of *Arena* and, with Desmond Egan, of *Choice*. He was also poetry editor of the *Irish Times* and a recipient of an American Fund Literary Award.

SEAMUS HEANEY (1939–)

Born in Derry, Heaney's bibliography is vast, his work encompassing poetry, criticism, theatre and translation. His major poetry collections are *Death of a Naturalist*, *Door Into the Dark*, *Wintering Out*, *North*, *Field Work*, *Selected Poems, 1965–1975*, *Poems, 1965–1975*, *Station Island*, *The Haw Lantern*, *New Selected Poems, 1966–1987*, *Seeing Things*, *The Spirit Level*, *The School Bag*, *Electric Light* and *Finders Keepers*. Along with Ted Hughes, he edited *The Rattle Bag*. His translation of *Beowulf* won him the Whitbread Book of the Year in 1999 and he was awarded the Nobel Prize for Literature in 1995. He is a former Professor of Poetry at Oxford University and currently Ralph Waldo Emerson Poet-in-Residence at Harvard.

JOHN HEWITT (1907–1987)

Born in Belfast and educated at Queens University, Hewitt worked in the art world all of his life. He began writing poetry in the 1920s and his first collection, *No Rebel Word*, was produced in 1948. He also established himself as a reviewer and art critic. In 1981 he was made a Freeman of the city of Belfast. Honorary doctorates were conferred upon him by the University of Ulster and Queens University Belfast. His lasting contribution to the arts in Ulster is celebrated at the John Hewitt International Summer School held each year in Garron Tower on the Antrim Coast.

F R HIGGINS (1896–1941)

Born in Co Mayo, Higgins was influenced by the Irish Literary Revival and became a close friend of both W B Yeats and Austin Clarke. He contributed reviews to the *Irish Statesman* and poetry to *The Dial*, *Spectator*, *Atlantic Monthly* and *Dublin Magazine*. He was also Director of the Abbey Theatre for a period and founding member and secretary of the Irish Academy of Letters. He published five volumes of poetry in his lifetime.

RITA ANN HIGGINS (1955–)

Born in Galway, where she still lives, Higgins's poetry collections are *Goddess on the Mervue Bus*, *Witch in the Bushes*, *Goddess and Witch*, *Philomena's Revenge*, *Higher Purchase*, *Sunny Side Plucked* and *An Awful Racket*. Her plays include *Face Licker Come Home*, *God of the Hatch Man* and *Down All the Roundabouts*. She has won several awards, including the Peadar O'Donnell Award, and her work has been selected for Yale University's Literature Curriculum.

PATRICK KAVANAGH (1904–1967)

Born in Inniskeen, Patrick Kavanagh's first volume of poems, *The Ploughman and Other Poems*, was published in 1936, with *The Green Fool* appearing two years later. He went to Dublin in 1939 and worked as a journalist. In the early forties his poems began to attract attention and one of the first to take note was Sir John Betjeman, later England's poet Laureate. The outline of Kavanagh's life in fictional form is portrayed in his novel *Tarry Flynn*, published in 1948. The novel was later made into a play and performed by the Abbey Theatre in Dublin and in Dundalk. Kavanagh died from pneumonia in 1967.

JOHN B KEANE (1928–2002)

Born in Listowel, Co Kerry, Keane published forty-six works. He is best known for his plays which include *Sive*, *Sharon's Grave*, *The Man from Clare*, *The Year of the Hiker*, *The Field* (which was adapted as a film of the same name), *Many Young Men of Twenty*, *Big Maggie*, *Moll*, *The Crazy Wall*, *The Buds of Ballybunion*, *The Chastitute* and *Faoiseamh*. His novels are *The Bodhran Makers*, *Durango*, *The Contractors* and *A High Meadow*. His biography is *Man of the Triple Name*. He was a former president of Irish PEN, an Honorary Life Member of the Royal Dublin Society, a D.Litt (hon.causa) Trinity College Dublin. He was also a founder member of the Society of Irish Playwrights.

RITA KELLY (1953–)

Born in Galway, Kelly's poetry collections are *An Bealach Eadóigh* and the bi-lingual *Fare Well: Beir Beannacht*. She has also published a short story collection entitled *The Whispering Arch and Other Stories*. With her late husband, Eoghan Ó Tuairisc, she published *Dialann sa Dísart*. She has won the Merriman Poetry Award and the Sean O'Riordain Memorial Prize for Poetry and was awarded an Arts Council/An Chomhairle Éalíon Bursary for Literature.

BRENDAN KENNELLY (1936–)

Kennelly achieved international recognition with his poem 'Cromwell', following this with the even more notorious *Book of Judas*, which topped the Irish bestsellers list. He has published over 20 other volumes of poetry as well as four verse plays, two novels and a substantial body of criticism. He is a renowned editor and anthologist, and is Professor of Modern Literature at Trinity College, Dublin.

THOMAS KETTLE (1880–1916)

Born in Co Dublin, the son of a founder of the Land League, Kettle grew up to be a nationalist poet, politician and soldier. He practiced law before becoming an MP and joined the Irish Volunteers prior to World War 1. He lost his life during the Battle of the Somme and his body was never recovered. Kettle's war journalism was posthumously published as *The Ways of War*.

THOMAS KINSELLA (1928–)

Born in Dublin, Kinsella's many collections of poems include *Another September*, *Downstream*, *Butcher's Dozen*, *Fifteen Dead*, *The Good Fight*, *Nightwalker and Other Poems*, *Notes from the Dead*, *One and Other Poems*, *Peppercanister Poems 1972–1978*, *St Catherine's Clock*, *Poems From City Centre* and *Madonna and Other Poems*. He has also edited *The New Oxford Book of Irish Verse*. His many awards include Guggenheim Fellowships and the Denis Devlin Memorial Award. He currently lives in Philadelphia.

EMILY LAWLESS (1845–1913)

Born in Co Kildare, Lawless published both novels and poems, including *A Millionaire's Cousin*, *Hurrish*, *With Essex in Ireland*, *Maelcho*, *Grania*, *Plain Frances Mowbray and Other Tales*, *Traits and Confidences* and *The Book of Gilly*. Her personal life was marred by tragedy with the suicide of her father and two sisters. She received a D.Litt. from Trinity College Dublin before her death in 1913.

FRANCIS LEDWIDGE (1891–1917)

Born in Slane, Co Meath, Ledwidge was a rural poet whose three volumes of poetry, *Songs of the Field*, *Songs of the Peace* and *Last Songs*, all celebrate the countryside. Ledwidge was killed in action in Flanders during World War 1. He is memorialised in Seamus Heaney's poem 'In Memoriam Francis Ledwidge'.

WINIFRED M LETTS (1882–1972)

Born in Co Wexford, Letts later moved to Kent. Her poems include *Songs from Leinster* and she was one of the few female poets to wrote about the effects of World War 1. She also wrote plays and novels, including *Christina's Son*, *The Eyes of the Blind*, *The Challenge*, *More Songs* and *Hallowe'en* and *Poems of the War*.

C DAY LEWIS (1904–1972)

Born at Ballintubber, Queen's County (now Co Laois), Lewis attended Oxford University and became part of the circle that gathered around W H Auden whom he helped to edit *Oxford Poetry* 1927. His own first collection of poems, *Beechen Virgil*, appeared in 1925. He was appointed Poet Laureate in 1968. He also gained fame as a detective story writer under the name Nicholas Blake. Lewis was married twice and fathered five children, one of whom is the Academy Award–winning actor Daniel Day-Lewis.

MICHAEL LONGLEY (1939–)

Born in Belfast, where he still lives, Longley was Writer Fellow at Trinity College Dublin in 1993. His works of poetry include *No Continuing, An Exploded View*, *Man Lying on a Wall*, *The Echo Gate*, *Poems 1963–1983*, *Poems 1963–1980*, *Gorse Fires*, for which he was awarded the 1991 Whitbread Prize for Poetry, *The Ghost Orchid*, *Broken Dishes*, *Selected Poems* and *The Weather in Japan*, for which he received the 2001 *Irish Times* Irish Literature Prize for Poetry. His most recent collection, *The Weather in Japan*, won both the Hawthornden Prize and the T. S. Eliot Prize. He was awarded the Queen's Gold Medal for Poetry in 2001 and is also a Fellow of the Royal Society of Literature. He lives in Belfast with his wife, the critic Edna Longley.

DONAGH MACDONAGH (1912–1968)

Born in Dublin, MacDonagh practised law, serving on the bench in Co Wexford for many years and as a judge in Dublin up to his death. He was also a broadcaster, poet and playwright, publishing *Twenty Poems* with Niall Sheridan and staging the first Irish production of *Murder in the Cathedral*. His ballad opera, *Happy as Larry*, was the most successful play in London in post-war years. His poems include 'The Hungry Grass' and 'Dublin Made Me'.

LOUIS MACNEICE (1907–1963)

Born in Belfast and brought up in Carrickfergus, Co Antrim, MacNeice studied Classics and Philosophy at Oxford and both of these subjects informed his poetry. He was reknowned as a translator, literary critic, playwright, autobiographer, BBC producer and feature writer as well as poet. His major works are *The Dark Tower*, *Roundabout Way* (written as Louis Malone), *Blind Fireworks*, *Poems*, *The Earth Compels*, *Autumn Journal*, *Plant and Phantom*, *Springboard*, *Holes in the Sky*, *Ten Burnt Offerings*, *Autumn Sequel*, *Visitations*, *Solstices*, *The Burning Perch* and *Persons from Porlock*.

DEREK MAHON (1941–)

Born in Belfast, Mahon's poetry collections include *Night–Crossing*, *The Snow Party*, *Poems 1962–1978*, *Courtyards in Delft*, *The Hunt By Night*, *Antarctica*, *The Yaddo Letter*, *The Yellow Book*, *The Hudson Letter* and *Collected Poems*. His translations include *The Chimeras*, *High Time*, *The Selected Poems of Philippe Jaccottet*, *The Bacchae of Euripedes* and Racine's *Phaedre*. His screenplays include *Summer Lightning* and his prose is collected as *Journalism*. His honours include the Irish American Foundation Award, a Lannan Foundation Award, a Guggenheim Fellowship, the *Irish Times*/Aer Lingus Poetry Prize, the American Ireland Fund Literary Award, the C.K. Scott Moncrieff Translation Prize, and the Eric Gregory Award. He lives in Dublin.

FRANCIS SYLVESTER MAHONY (1804–1866)

Also known under the pseudonym Father Prout, Mahony was born in Cork and educated at a Jesuit college in Amiens. He studied and taught in Paris and Rome, but later moved to London where he wrote for *Fraser's Magazine* and kept the company of writers such as Coleridge and Thackeray. He was persuaded by Charles Dickens to become Rome correspondent for *The Daily News* in 1849 and also acted as *Globe* correspondent in Paris. His writings are issued as *The Works of Father Prout*.

MEDBH MCGUCKIAN (1950–)

Born in Belfast in 1950, McGuckian's collections of poetry include *The Flower Master*, *Venus and the Rain*, *On Ballycastle Beach*, *Marconi's Cottage*, *Captain Lavender*, *Selected Poems*, *Drawing Ballerinas* and *The Face of the Earth*. Her awards include the Cheltenham Award, the Alice Hunt Bartlett Prize, and the Bass Ireland Award for Literature in 1991. *Marconi's Cottage* was shortlisted for the *Irish Times*/Aer Lingus Irish Literature Prize for Poetry.

FRANK MCGUINNESS (1953–)

Born in Buncrana, Co Donegal, McGuinness's plays include *The Factory Girls*, *Baglady/Ladybag*, *Observe the Sons of Ulster Marching Towards the Somme*, *Innocence*, *Carthaginians*, *Mary and Lizzie*, *The Bread Man*, *Someone Who'll Watch Over Me* and *Dolly West's Kitchen*. He has adapted Ibsen's *Rosmersholm* and *Peer Gynt*, Chekov's *Three Sisters* and Brecht's *The Threepenny Opera*. He has also written for television, including *Scout* and *The Hen House*. His awards include the London *Evening Standard* Award for Most Promising Playwright, the Prix de l'Intervision and the Prix de l'Art Critique. His poetry collections are *Booterstown* and *The Sea With No Ships*. He lives in County Dublin.

PAULA MEEHAN (1955–)

Born in Dublin, Meehan studied at Trinity College where she was Writer Fellow in the English Department. Her poetry collections include *Return and No Blame*, *Reading the Sky*, *The Man Who Was Marked by Winter*, which was shortlisted for the *Irish Times*/Aer Lingus Irish Literature Prize for Poetry, *Pillow Talk*, which was shortlisted for the *Irish Times* Literature Prize for Poetry, *Mysteries of the Home: A Selection of Poems* and *Dharmakaya*. She has also written plays for children and adults, including *Mrs Sweeney* and *Cell*. She has been awarded the Marten Toonder

Prize by the Arts Council and the Butler Award for Poetry by the Irish American Cultural Institute. She lives in Dublin.

JOHN MONTAGUE (1929–)

Born in Brooklyn, New York, but reared on the family farm in Co Tyrone, Montague's poetry includes *Forms of Exile*, *Poisoned Lands*, *A Chosen Light*, *Tides; The Rough Field*, *A Slow Dance*, *The Great Cloak*, *The Dead Kingdom*, *Mount Eagle*, *The Love Poems*, *Time in Armagh*, *Collected Poems* and *Smashing the Piano*. His fiction includes *The Lost Notebook* and the short stories *An Occasion of Sin*. He has edited *Bitter Harvest*, an anthology of Irish poetry. Among numerous prizes and honours, he has received the American Ireland Fund Literary Award. He lives in Co Cork.

PAUL MULDOON (1951–)

Born in Portadown in Co Armagh, Muldoon read English at Queen's University Belfast. While he was at university Faber published his first collection of poems, *New Weather*. For several years he was a radio producer for BBC Northern Ireland. He moved to the USA in 1987 and has held various university teaching posts, most recently Director of the Creative Writing Program at Princeton University, where he is Howard G. B. Clark Professor in the Humanities. In 1999 he was elected Professor of Poetry at Oxford University. He has won many awards and prizes, including the Geoffrey Faber Memorial Prize in 1991, the T S Eliot Award, the American Academy of Arts and Letters Award for Literature in 1996, and the *Irish Times* Irish Literature Prize.

RICHARD MURPHY (1927–)

Born in Mayo, Murphy's poetry collections include *The Archaeology of Love*, *Sailing to an Island*, *The Battle of Aughrim*, *High Island*, *High Island: New and Selected Poems*, *The Price of Stone*, *The Mirror Wall* and *In The Heart Of The Country: Collected Poems*. His awards include the AE Memorial Award, two British Arts Council Awards, the Marten Toonder Award and the American–Irish Foundation Award. He is also a

Fellow of the Royal Society of Literature. Murphy lives in Co Dublin.

DENNIS O'DRISCOLL (1954–)

Born in Thurles, Co Tipperary, O'Driscoll is a former editor of *Poetry Ireland Review*, and one of Ireland's most widely published and respected critics of poetry. He has published several collections – *Kist*, *Hidden Extras*, *Long Story Short*, *The Bottom Line*, *Quality Time*, *Weather Permitting*, which was a London Poetry Book Society Recommendation and for which he was awarded the Lannan Poetry Prize, and *Exemplary Damages*. A selection from his *Pickings and Cuttings* column of poetry quotations, *As The Poet Said*, was published by Poetry Ireland in 1997. His prose writing is collected as *Troubled Thoughts, Majestic Dreams: Selected Prose Writings*. He lives in Co Kildare.

FRANK ORMSBY (1947–)

Born in Enniskillen, Co Fermanagh, Ormsby was educated at Queen's University Belfast. He is Head of English at the Royal Belfast Academical Institution. His books of poetry include *Ripe for Company*, *A Store of Candles*, *A Northern Spring* and *The Ghost Train*. He has also edited a number of anthologies, including *Thine in Storm and Calm: An Amanda McKittrick Ros Reader*, *The Collected Poems of John Hewitt* and *Northern Windows: An Anthology of Ulster Autobiography*. Most recently he has edited *The Hip Flask: Short Poems from Ireland*. In 1992 he received the Cultural Traditions Award, given in memory of John Hewitt, and in 2002 the Lawrence O'Shaughnessy Award for Poetry from the University of St Thomas at St Paul, Minnesota.

ARTHUR O'SHAUGHNESSY (1844–1881)

O'Shaughnessy's working life, from 1861 to his death, was spent as an assistant in the British Museum. He was a friend of Rossetti and of Ford Madox Brown and married the sister of another poet, Philip Bourke Marston. French poetry was his prevailing influence and his volumes of poetry include *An Epic of Women*, *Lays of France* and *Music and Moonlight*. His most enduring poem, known from its

first line, 'We are the music makers,' was later set to music by Edward Elgar and Zoltán Kodály. O'Shaughnessy married Eleanor Marston in 1873, with whom he wrote *Toy–land*, a book of children's stories.

PADRAIC PEARSE (1879–1916)

Pearse was born in Dublin, received his education from the Christian Brothers, and completed a degree in Arts and Law at the Royal University in 1901. His interest in the Irish language led Pearse to join the Gaelic League and he became editor of its paper. Initially in his political career Pearse was a moderate, but he soon conceived the idea that independence could only be achieved by force and sacrifice. Pearse was recruited into the IRB in 1912 and later became a member of the Military Council of the organisation. He was president of the Provisional Government and was stationed in the GPO during the Rising. He was executed in Kilmainham Gaol in 1916.

JOSEPH MARY PLUNKETT (1887–1916)

Plunkett worked as director of the Irish Theatre and co–editor of the *Irish Review* and had close ties with the literary world. He was a member of the Military Council of the Provisional Government and the Provisional Committee of the Irish Volunteers and was a major figure in the 1916 Rebellion, along with Michael Collins. He married artist Grace Gifford in Kilhmainham Gaol just hours before his execution.

DAVID QUIN

Born in Dublin's Rotunda, Quin wrote the first thesis (as far as is known) on Seamus Heaney and has worked as a journalist with *Hibernia Review*, *Sunday Tribune* and the *Irish Independent*. He is now course leader of the MA in Journalism at the Dublin Institute of Technology. He won second prize in the OZ Whitehead Play Competition in 2001. 'Pity the Islanders' won the National Poetry Prize in 1992.

CATHAL Ó SEARCAIGH (1956–)

Born in Donegal, Ó Searcaigh lives at the foot of Mount Errigal. His collections of poetry include *Homecoming/An Bealach 'na Bhaile* and *Na Buachaillí Bána* and *An Tnúth leis an tSolas*, for which he received the *Irish Times* Irish Literature Prize for the Irish language. His plays include *Mairimid leis na Mistéirí Tá an Tóin at Titim as an tSaol* and *Ghealaí*, based on the story of Salomé. He has been awarded the Seán Ó Ríordáin Prize for Poetry and the Duais Bhord na Gaeilge.

JAMES SIMMONS (1933–2001)

Born in Derry, Simmons moved to London before taking a degree at the University of Leeds. He edited *Poetry and Audience* with fellow–students Wole Soyinka and Tony Harrison and went on to publish a number of collections, including *In the Wilderness, The Long Summer Still to Come, Constantly Singing* and *The Company of Children*. He was also the founding editor of *The Honest Ulsterman*, which showcased early writing by Paul Muldoon, Frank Ormsby and Bernard MacLaverty. His awards include the Cholmondeley Poetry Award and the Irish Publishers' Award and he was Writer in Residence at Queen's University 1985–1988. He also founded The Poet's House in Co Antrim) which offered a curriculum actively supported by Seamus Heaney, Paul Durcan and Carol Ann Duffy among others.

PETER SIRR (1960–)

Born in Waterford, Sirr won the Patrick Kavanagh Award in 1982 and the poetry prize at Listowel Writers' Week the following year. His collections of poetry are *Marginal Zones, Talk, Talk, Ways of Falling, The Ledger of Fruitful Exchange* and *Bring Everything*. He is director of the Irish Writers' Centre and lives in Dublin.

JAMES STEPHENS (1882–1950)

A poet, playwright and author, Stephens was also a passionate nationalist and incorporated Irish folklore into his work. During the 1920s he met and became good friends with James Joyce. Among his works are *Insurrections, The Charwoman's Daughter, The Demi Gods, Deirdre* and *In the Land of Youth*.

J M SYNGE (1871–1909)

Synge was born near Dublin and received his degree from Trinity College Dublin before going to Germany to study music and later to Paris, where he lived for several years. There, he met a compatriot, William Butler Yeats, who persuaded Synge to live in the Aran Islands and then return to Dublin and devote himself to creative work. *The Aran Islands* is the journal of Synge's retreat among these primitive people. The plays of Irish peasant life on which his fame rests were written in the last six years of his life and include *In the Shadow of the Glen* and *The Playboy of the Western World*.

OSCAR WILDE (1854–1900)

Having attended Trinity College Dublin and Oxford University, where he excelled in his studies and won prizes for his poetry, Wilde moved to London where he published his first volume of poetry in 1881. On a trip to the United States, he met fellow poets Walt Whitman and Henry Longfellow, and returned to London to write poems, plays and his first and only novel, *The Picture of Dorian Gray*. His notably successful plays include *Lady Windermere's Fan* and *The Importance of Being Earnest*, which earned him critical and commercial success. In 1895, Wilde was arrested because of his relationship with Lord Alfred Douglas and was sentenced to two years' imprisonment. His long poem *The Ballad of Reading Gaol* is an account of his experiences in prison. He died of meningitis three years after his release.

FLORENCE WILSON (1870–1946)

Born in Co Antrim, Wilson was a contributor to *Irish Homestead, Northern Whig* and other papers, and an associate of Alice Milligan and A S Green. As well as the author of the ballad 'The Man from God Knows Where', she also published a poetry collection entitled *The Coming of the Earls*.

MACDARA WOODS (1942–)

Born in Dublin, Woods's collections of poetry include *Decimal D. Sec Drinks in a Bar in Marrakesh, Early Morning Matins, Stopping the Lights in Ranelagh, Miz Moon, The Hanged Man Was Not Surrendering, Notes From the Country of Blood–Red Flowers, The Nightingale Water* and *Knowledge in the Blood*. He lives in Dublin.

W B YEATS (1865–1939)

Born in Dublin, Yeats was educated there and in London. The young Yeats was very much part of the *fin de siècle* in London, but at the same time he was active in societies that attempted an Irish literary revival. His first volume of verse appeared in 1887, but in his earlier period his dramatic production outweighed his poetry both in bulk and in import. Together with Lady Gregory he founded the Irish Theatre, which was to become the Abbey Theatre, and served as its chief playwright until the movement was joined by J M Synge. His plays include *The Countess Cathleen, The Land of Heart's Desire, Cathleen ni Houlihan, The King's Threshold* and *Deirdre*. He was appointed to the Irish Senate in 1922 and he also received the Nobel Prize, chiefly for his dramatic works. His poetry includes the volumes *The Wild Swans at Coole, Michael Robartes and the Dancer, The Tower, The Winding Stair and Other Poems* and *Last Poems and Plays*.

Index of First Lines

Index of Poets and Poems

Acknowledgements

Special thanks to

Pat Balfe
Tom Barton
Suzie Bateman
John Bateson
Gordon Bolton
Jane Bolton
Pat Boran
Eimear Bradley
Amanda Brown
Richard Burke
Tony Byrne
Pierce Casey
Maurice Cassidy
Carol Coleman
Denise Conway
Amy Corrigan
Tom Costello
Deirdre Costello
John Cunningham
Noel Cusack
Jane Dalton
John Dardis
Anne Dargan
Denis Desmond
Liz Devlin
Theo Dorgan
Angela Douglas
Claire Doyle
Nigel Duke
Pat Dunne
Pat Egan
Ursula Fanning

Brian Farrell
Claudine Farrell
Rachel Fehily
Christine Fitzpatrick
Cyril Freaney
Barbara Galavan
Barry Gaster
Anita Gibney
Liam Giles
Justin Green
Brian Hand
Patricia Hanson
Jared Harris
Noel Harris
Shay Healy
Colin Henry
Caroline Hickson
Lindsay Holmes
Siobhan Hough
John Hughes
Ros and John Hubbard
Susan Hunter
Declan Jones
Helina Kearney
Steve Kenis
Brendan Kennelly
Peter Kenny
Joe King
Philip King
Kathy Kruse-Kennedy
David Landsman
Johnny Lappin
Paul Lenehan

Marty Miller
Eamon McCann
John McColgan
Alastair McGuckian
Cathal McLysaght
Yvonne McMahon
Avila Molloy
Mark Molloy
Nikki Molloy
Joe Moreau
Mike Murphy
Fiona Nagle
Bill O'Donovan
Fred O'Donovan
Dennis O'Driscoll
Jack O'Leary
Willie O'Reilly
Tom Owen
Lucia Proctor
John Redmond
Jean Reilly
Sara Ryan
John Sheehan
Dave Slevin
Norma Smurfit
Colin Stokes
Claire Strudwick
Joe Woods
Caitriona Ward
Paddy White
Philip Wood